'Producers are the backbone of a movie industry and this book perfectly chronicles the challenges faced by movie producers.'

—*Arya, actor and producer*

'The Indian movie industry encompasses South, North, East and Western regions of India and it is much more than just Bollywood. I am glad that this book takes a holistic view and presents the span and depth of this industry.'

—*Katragadda Prasad, President, South Indian Film Chamber of Commerce*

'In the past two decades, by organising the Chennai International Film Festival, we have successfully placed Chennai on the world map of cinema. This book takes a step forward in recording the cinema legacy of Chennai and pointing to its historical significance.'

—*Emanadar Thangaraj, Festival Director, Chennai International Film Festival*

'Born and brought up in the amazing world of Indian cinema, for me it is riveting to read the incredibly challenging journey of a film entrepreneur that is captured very well in this book.'

—*Sanjay Wadhwa, third-generation movie entrepreneur,*
financier, distributor and content aggregator

T0271984

INDIAN MOVIE ENTREPRENEURSHIP

One of the world's most prolific creative industries, the Indian movie industry has received scant attention for its spirit of enterprise. *Indian Movie Entrepreneurship* addresses this omission.

For many readers, it might come as a surprise that the Indian movie industry is not just Bollywood and that it has several regional clusters, which are just as vibrant, with a significant output. The authors begin by outlining the contours of Indian cinema and the different regional language hubs that form part of the larger picture. The reader is then offered a glimpse into the actual process of making a film from day zero to release day. The key players in the Indian movie ecosystem are analysed, with the central role of the producer highlighted. Concluding with a look into the future of the entrepreneurial process in the Indian movie industry, the authors illuminate the shifting parameters of distribution and exhibition.

Appealing to those interested in understanding the entrepreneurial journey of the Indian movie industry, the book provides a sneak peek into the business landscape of India more broadly.

Rajeev Kamineni was actively involved in the production, marketing and business development of 14 movies in the Indian movie industry. He was a member of the board of the Indo Cine Appreciation Foundation (ICAF), and an organising committee member of the Chennai International Film Festival (CIFF).

Ruth Rentschler OAM has more than 20 years' experience in services, arts and cultural management; and leadership in hospitality, the creative industries and academia. She has similar experience working in governance, management and marketing in the non-profit sphere at local, state, national and international levels. She was Head of the School of Management and Professor of Arts and Cultural Leadership at the University of South Australia.

MASTERING MANAGEMENT IN THE CREATIVE AND CULTURAL INDUSTRIES

Series Editor: Ruth Rentschler

Creative and cultural industries account for a significant share of the global economy. Gaining and maintaining employment and work in this sector is a challenge and chances of success are enhanced by ongoing professional development.

This series provides a range of relatively short, student-centred books which blend business management expertise with cultural sector practice. Books in the series provide either an arts applied introduction to a particular business discipline, or a business management lens through which to understand a key segment of the arts world. In sum, the series provides essential reading for those studying to enter the creative industries as well as those seeking to enhance their career via executive education.

Titles in this series include:

Artist Management: Agility in the Creative and Cultural Industries
Guy Morrow

Visual Arts Management
Jeffrey Taylor

Managing Organizations in the Creative Economy: Organizational Behaviour for the Cultural Sector
Paul Saintilan and David Schreiber

Strategic Analysis: A Creative and Cultural Industries Perspective
Jonathan Gander

Indian Movie Entrepreneurship: Not Just Song and Dance
Rajeev Kamineni and Ruth Rentschler

For more information about this series, please visit: www.routledge.com/Mastering-Management-in-the-Creative-and-Cultural-Industries/book-series/MMCCI

INDIAN MOVIE ENTREPRENEURSHIP

Not Just Song and Dance

Rajeev Kamineni and Ruth Rentschler

Routledge
Taylor & Francis Group

LONDON AND NEW YORK

First published 2020
by Routledge
2 Park Square, Milton Park, Abingdon, Oxon OX14 4RN

and by Routledge
52 Vanderbilt Avenue, New York, NY 10017

Routledge is an imprint of the Taylor & Francis Group, an informa business

British Library Cataloguing-in-Publication Data
A catalogue record for this book is available from the British Library

Library of Congress Cataloging-in-Publication Data
A catalog record has been requested for this book

ISBN: 978-1-138-39383-7 (hbk)
ISBN: 978-1-138-39381-3 (pbk)
ISBN: 978-0-429-40153-4 (ebk)

Typeset in Bembo
by Swales & Willis, Exeter, Devon, UK

To the three ladies in my life: Amma, Priya and Ahalya—RK

To my dearest Geoffrey, Anna and James—RR

CONTENTS

AUTHORS

Rajeev Kamineni has been actively involved in the production, marketing and business development of 14 movies in the Indian movie industry. He has been a member of the board of the Indo Cine Appreciation Foundation (ICAF), and an organising committee member of the Chennai International Film Festival (CIFF).

Rajeev brings deep, first-hand knowledge of the Indian movie business through his involvement in the financing, production, marketing and business development of movies. He is a key member of the producers' circle across South India. He knows the stars, the senior producers and the crew who make Indian movies such a success (and sometimes a failure). These people gave their time with nothing to gain on their part, other than to support Rajeev. Hence, this book captures his journey as much as it captures that of the producers and their circle. Rajeev's contribution adds authenticity to the story because of his experience. This book is more than just another research project. It is a personal testament to the journey of one individual woven into the stories of many others.

Ruth Rentschler OAM has more than 20 years' experience in services, arts and cultural management; and leadership in hospitality, the creative industries and academia. She has similar experience working in governance, management and marketing in the non-profit sphere at local, state, national and international levels. She was Head of the School of Management and Professor of Arts and Cultural Leadership at the University of South Australia.

Professor Rentschler (BA Hons Melbourne, PhD Monash) has considerable experience as an entrepreneur, starting her own business in services which she ran for ten years, as well as researching in entrepreneurship in cultural and creative industries. She also has a long-standing interest in Asia and indeed India, where she has travelled widely as an academic. Ruth is a member of the JLF Executive Advocacy Group for the Adelaide Festival Centre and works closely as a facilitator with JLF during its OzAsia presence in Adelaide. She has published widely and won multiple awards in academia for her supervision, grant prowess and community engagement. She has been awarded the Medal for the Order of Australia (OAM). Under the broad heading of diversity, her research interests are at the micro-level in cultural entrepreneurship and arts governance. She retains a keen interest in movies and the movie business.

ACKNOWLEDGEMENTS

The movie industry created a lasting impression for principal author Rajeev, who grew up in a town in Southern India. The two main career interests and 'exports' from this region are movies and politics. For better or worse, he escaped the lure of politics, but could not move away from the fascination for the arc lights and silver screen. As a business choice, movie production is a risky new venture, due to its exceptionally high rate of failure: fewer than 20 per cent of movies released every year can be termed a success. In the movie industry it feels like failure is a constant, whereas success is the exception. During the course of this project, interactions with producers who have declared bankruptcy and were going through emotional breakdowns was an eye-opener, as were reports of producers who have committed suicide and the devastating consequences on their families and employees. As authors, this motivated us to understand the psyche of a movie producer. Despite so many examples of failure, despite the odds being heavily stacked against producers, why does an individual decide to pursue movie production?

A book on the Indian movie industry is a challenging project to undertake due to the inherent complexities in one of the world's largest entertainment industries, and the prevalence of specific viewpoints, stereotypes and misconceptions. However, this book was possible because of the warmth and genuine spirit of cooperation exhibited by several stakeholders in the Indian movie industry. Despite busy schedules and impending release deadlines, all were most accommodating and granted our requests, even on short notice. Chronicling the entrepreneurial journey of Indian movie producers would not have been possible if not for the central characters in this plot—the producers themselves—wholeheartedly sharing their experiences and placing their trust in us to present their story.

Hearty thanks to a dear friend, Mr Jamshad Arya, for his time and swift permission to use the figures in this book. Special thanks to Mr Vinay Chilakapati, a fellow traveller and friend for three decades. We express gratitude to and acknowledge the assistance of colleagues, team members and friends: Mr VR Arasu, Mr SP Sankar, Mr Kishore and Mr Naren. Continuous encouragement and support from Mr Sanjay Wadhwa is much appreciated. It was truly a humbling experience to spend considerable time with legends Mr AVM Saravanan and Mr SP Muthuraman. Sincere thanks to Mr MS Guhan for facilitating this meeting and helping us with research material. Thanks to Ms Subha J Rao, Mr Kalyanam, Mr A Sreekar Prasad and Mr E Thangaraj for moral support, sharing anecdotes and a passion for cinema. Sincere thanks to producers: Mr L Suresh, Mr Katragadda Prasad, Late Mr Shanmugam, Mr Sathya Jyothi Thyagarajan, Mr Kalaipuli Thanu, Mr Ravi Kottarakara, Mr Lakshman Kumar, Mr SR Prabhu, Mr KE Gnanavel Raja, Mr S Sashikanth, Mr Raj Kumar, Mr C Kalyan, Mr Krishna Reddy, Mr G Dhananjayan, Mr Subbu, Mr CV Kumar, Mr Amma Siva, Mr Suresh Balaje, Mr M Balasubramaniam, Mrs Kameela Nasser and Mr Tatineni Rama Rao.

Sincere thanks to Professor Gus Geursen for advising on the entrepreneurial focus of this book. Special thanks to Dr Martine Hawkes for patiently reading through the manuscript several times and ironing out many wrinkles. Thanks to Ms Avninder Aydee for her time and patience in reviewing the manuscript with a fresh set of eyes. We are extremely grateful to our universities, The University of Adelaide and the University of South Australia, for the opportunity to pursue this topic, through which the next generation of entrepreneurs may be taught the concepts presented and be influenced to take up the mantle of movie entrepreneurship in the future.

PREFACE

One of the world's most prolific creative industries, the Indian movie industry has received scant attention for its spirit of entrepreneurship and business management. This book is positioned towards a reader base interested in business and entrepreneurship in general, and towards students, researchers and trade analysts of cinema in particular. Though cinema falls under the broad category of cultural and creative industries, its impact on the social milieu is pronounced. Therefore, this book is for those who are, or who would like to be, employed within the media and entertainment industry, as they seek to carve out a career.

Exponents of international business have listed the challenges of doing business in Asia and India. The Indian movie industry is a microcosm of India and offers a fascinating insight into the complexities of navigating through the maze of regulations, handshake deals, lack of transparency, low-entry barriers and the high failure rate. In a way, understanding the entrepreneurial journey of the Indian movie industry is akin to getting a sneak peek into the business landscape of India.

For many readers, it might come as a surprise that Indian cinema is not just Bollywood; it has several regional clusters, which are just as vibrant, with a significant movie output. This book starts off by explaining the contours of Indian cinema and the different regional language hubs that form part of the larger picture. The reader is then offered a glimpse into the actual process of making a movie from day zero to release day, and also to appreciate the ten key players in the Indian movie ecosystem, with the central role of the producer highlighted. We also cover the three key aspects of the entrepreneurial process: opportunity recognition; team formation; and resource allocation—all of which are analysed within the specific context of the Indian movie industry. The book concludes with a glimpse into the future of the entrepreneurial process in the

Indian movie industry, especially with a view to the shifting parameters of digital and streaming platforms.

A major challenge in writing a book about movies is that it is a popular medium where everyone likes to have an opinion. This is more pronounced in the case of Indian cinema where movies have an image of singing and dancing that caters to the basic senses of the audience but contains limited intellectual content. The title of this book lends itself to that prejudice by portraying the Indian movie industry as more than just singing and dancing! But the place of entrepreneurship is also where failure is common and success is hard to achieve. Another crucial point addressed in the book is whether to call the Indian movie industry a cultural industry or a creative industry. It can be both, we argue. For us, the emphasis should be on the industry component: an industry where livelihoods are created, employment generated, and that contributes to the growth of the national economy as well as the national identity.

INTRODUCTION

Why India?

In this book we examine the Indian movie industry. There is a dearth of research on entrepreneurs in the movie industry in general, and the Indian movie industry in particular, despite its significant cultural and economic contribution. Hence, there are three key reasons for choosing to examine the Indian movie industry.

First, a focus on one of the fastest growing economies' movie industry can benefit not only leaders and managers, policymakers and scholars, fans and producers, but also entrepreneurs and entrepreneurship itself, all of which are central to a movie's success, as well as being the topic of our book. We see our book as laying down foundations and principles for the long-term viability of the Indian movie industry. The moviemaking business is risky. It is more likely to be successful for independent Indian producers if they develop adequate skills through formal training, or a certificate or apprenticeship in at least two projects before producing a movie. As highlighted by Ernst and Young in 2019, the Indian national skills network—the Federation of Indian Chambers of Commerce and Industry (FICCI)—with funding from the National Skill Development Corporation (NSDC), is setting up and promoting a skill development council specifically for the media and entertainment industry. The clear mandate for this council is to create a 1.2 million strong skilled workforce by 2022 in the media and entertainment sector across 74 job profiles. Fortunately, both line producer and executive producer are listed in those 74 profiles (Media and Entertainment Skills Council). It is a positive start that will help in training because the natural career progression for a line and executive producer is towards the role of full producer. This initiative will address the functional skills gap. However, the bigger challenge of filling the entrepreneurial skills gap needs to be addressed. Entrepreneurial skills pertaining to managing the business risks, building a team and identifying sources of funding need to be imparted to new and aspiring producers. For producers who shift from different sectors into the movie sector, this might not be a major hurdle because the basic entrepreneurial skills can be transferred between sectors. Entrepreneurial education and training skills programmes are available at several government-funded as well as privately managed institutions across India (Roy and Mukherjee 2017). Indian producers are, we argue, entrepreneurial, taking great risks in order to bring movies to the screen. We envisage our book exemplifying an approach that will encourage others to take entrepreneurship research forward in this rapidly growing field of the subcontinent.

It is vital to create a supportive environment that can assist existing and potential Indian movie producers. One of the challenges that confronts a new movie producer is lack of funding sources due to the restrictions placed by the Reserve Bank of India. Public sector banks are hesitant to finance movie projects unless strong collateral is offered as security. Private sector banks follow the guidelines of the public sector banks so as to reduce their exposure to non-performing assets. This forces Indian movie producers to approach independent financiers who charge exorbitant rates of interest. An interest rate of 36 per cent per annum is par for the course in the Indian movie industry. Therefore, for budding entrepreneurs to choose cinema production as a pathway for their entrepreneurial ambition, it is essential that it should be easy to obtain start-up funding. Additionally, many Indian movie producers do not understand how private equity and venture capital funding operates or the process for tapping into those funds. This lack of awareness results in poorly prepared pitch documents and a high rate of rejection as applicants have not exhibited investor readiness by alleviating the risk concerns of lenders and investors. Training existing and aspiring movie producers in the formal procedure of raising both debt and equity capital will help to cultivate a professional approach and open up the Indian movie industry to access wider sources of funding. It might also be beneficial for the investors and venture capitalists to be trained about the operational details of the Indian movie industry so they are better prepared to mitigate risk and appreciate the growth, maturity and decline in the business cycle. A start has been made on this front and it will gather momentum.

Second, there is a need to assess the directions and scope of the Indian movie industry, as many critical matters remain unexamined. Most books on the Indian movie industry focus on the movies themselves, their stars, or Bollywood as the generator of fantasies and fun. We go behind the camera to examine the independent Indian movie producer, who has been mostly overlooked but is central to movie success. Our goal is to share insights into the movie industry in order to stimulate interest relevant to leaders and managers, policymakers and scholars, as well as movie fans and, of course, the producers who are central to our story. As Eliashberg, Elberse and Leenders (2006) found in examining the Hollywood movie industry, the evolution of the movie industry, perceptions of producers and the role of the entrepreneurial producer need to be at the forefront of scholarly work. This book starts to provide some of those answers.

Third, the Indian movie industry is widely popular across the world, and global citizens are aware of the industry, though may lack an in-depth understanding of the intricate financial dealings within. Previously, there were several hurdles and restrictions on Indian entrepreneurs accessing capital from outside India, but this has changed significantly in the past decade. Indian movie entrepreneurs should now aim for global acceptability and access, given that many of the controls have been removed or eased to facilitate the entrepreneurial process. Whatever gaps existed in obtaining start-up and development funds from local Indian financial institutions have been bridged by being able to access overseas capital. Moving in the direction of intellectual internationalisation (Geursen and Dana 2001), Reliance, an Indian business conglomerate, has a partnership with Steven Spielberg's DreamWorks (Govil 2009). It has not yet yielded the expected results or paved the way for other Indian entertainment companies to operate on the global stage, but it is just a matter of time.

It is only recently that networking and mentoring have started to be encouraged. Indian family businesses play a significant role in this respect (Garg and Parikh 1986), with the examples of Rajshri, Yash Raj, Dharma and AVM illustrating the importance of mentoring. Yet in all these examples, mentoring was performed by the founder and passed down to the next generation, which had been actively groomed by the founder. In some situations, however, family businesses restricted themselves to certain pockets of influence, not professionalising their enterprise or enabling the business to continue following the demise of the founder's family or a lack of involvement in day-to-day management. Indian movie companies should view the Walt Disney Corporation as a role model in this respect. Fortunately, the Indian movie industry has always valued the role of formalised networking associations like the Producers Guild of India, Movie Federation of India and South Indian film Chamber of Commerce that focus on the exchange of ideas among movie entrepreneurs, capital providers, creative professionals, artists and technicians. Though these bodies are not funded by the government, they are valued as representatives of the industry and their inputs sought when making policy decisions. Therefore, these industry bodies can use their credibility and clout to ensure that new entrants into the industry are mentored and supported.

Focus of this book

This book is based on the Indian independent movie producer's entrepreneurial journey. It examines a field of endeavour that has been largely neglected. It has three important dimensions. First, the historical dimension in which the economic and social aspects of moviemaking and its importance to a developing country is seen to change over time. If we take the last seven decades as our time scale, the Indian movie industry has grown sharply. The industry is of great economic importance to the state, with the movie business predicted to grow by 7.7 per cent due to overseas expansion, growing regional content and digital streams (KPMG India 2017). The Central Board of Film Certification (CBFC 2017) certified 1,986 movies produced in India in the year 2017, significantly higher than the 700 produced in the USA. By 2016, India was producing 694 movies from Mumbai alone, with the top 50 movies contributing around 96 per cent of the box office (KPMG India 2017). In 2018, movies generated over 175 billion Rupees (EY 2019), with regional movie successes growing to 50 per cent of the domestic market. The Indian movie industry is talent-driven, with a few leading men and women dominating the market, but opportunities for new talent grow as more content emerges (KPMG India 2017). The US$24 billion (EY 2019) media and entertainment industry in India is expanding rapidly with significant revenue contribution from ancillary sales, such as those to Netflix. Movies drive the market for entertainment products as a key export industry. All these activities develop buzz around a movie, its entrepreneurial development and release to audiences.

Second, there is an increasing focus on entrepreneurship in the Indian movie industry (KPMG India 2017). As advertisers take advantage of innovation in moviemaking and the opportunity to advertise, exhibitors provide more opportunities to promote products and services. Further, movies have high cultural significance, attracting wide attention. Unlike other entertainment products, box office sales are frequently reported in the media. Research highlighting the manner in which producers of Indian movies respond to changes as the industry grows and their entrepreneurial practices develop has also been neglected. Previous books on Indian movies have focused on actors or movies themselves rather than on the producer. The cluster of movie companies centred around Mumbai on the west coast of India alone is bigger than Hollywood in the USA (Lorenzen and Täube 2008). The Indian cinema, with its Bollywood branding, is well-known internationally, commercially successful and operates without state subsidy for both big and small budget movies, as producers pursue blockbusters (Elberse 2013). Annual turnover in the movie industry is US$38.6 billion globally, projected to reach US$50 billion by 2020, and employs over 2 million people in the USA alone (MPAA 2017). Yet, fewer than 20 per cent of movies are successful (Sparviero 2015), so entrepreneurial failure is pervasive in this industry.

Third, entrepreneurial expression of the art form of Indian movies embraces business and creativity in order to see movies succeed in domestic and international markets. A great deal of data is available on movies. Nonetheless, most of that research has been undertaken on movies in the USA, followed by Europe and the UK. Much of the research has been from an economic perspective, focusing on celebrity star power, ticket sales, revenue, financial success and audiences (e.g., Litman and Kohl 1989; Wallace, Seigerman and Holbrook 1993; Prag and Casavant 1994; Ravid 1999). Movies rely on traditional stories and conventional wisdom—simple rules of thumb for their success—but are now in an environment of change, with digital demand pushing the boundaries (Eliashberg, Elberse and Leenders 2006). Insights into the film industry as a key service industry may expand understanding of the entrepreneurial behaviour of an industry in a developing nation that could provide lessons for the movie industry in other countries.

This book focuses on the independent producer and their entrepreneurial journey, which includes the role of distribution and exhibition, as well as generating audiences, in movie success. We are showcasing the entrepreneurial role of the producer. Nonetheless, we briefly provide an overview of other stages but exclude ancillary modes such as DVD sales, pay-TV and online streaming. Distributors, exhibitors and actors can also be entrepreneurs, as shall be alluded to in our chapters, but this is outside the scope of the book.

Evidence for this book

This book is underpinned by a review of the literature, both academic and popular, despite the dearth of material regarding the Indian independent movie producer. However, it is also enriched by interviews of Indian movie producers and other stakeholders, whose reponses are presented verbatim. We also conducted additional informal conversations with stakeholders in various locations as and when opportunities arose. For example, interviews and conversations were conducted in India, in the main, although some additional conversations were held in other locations during festivals, and as part of an engagement with the Indian diaspora around the world. The credibility of the authors is bolstered by the fact that the lead author spent considerable time enriching his understanding of the contemporary Indian movie marketplace having been a movie professional, developer, creator and writer. The lead author possesses wide-ranging experience in the Indian movie industry, giving authenticity to the stories of the movie entrepreneurial process narrated from the producers' perspectives in this book. Ruth Rentschler was the Master of Ceremony at an Indian literary and movie festival where she met many high-profile individuals from the Indian movie industry, which enriched her understanding of the eco-system. Together, their experiences of the entertainment and creative industries in general, and movies from India and beyond in particular, provide a rich texture for the book.

Structure of this book

This book was conceived to present the entrepreneurial nature of the Indian movie industry and to provide a historical context and detail the current stage to which the Indian movie industry has evolved. The first part of the book details the evolution of the Indian movie business. Chapter 1 presents evidence of the need for this book; Chapter 2 deals with the different major industries of Indian cinema and the producers' role in shaping them. The second part of the book presents Indian movie producers' perceptions about the business. Chapter 3 details the role of a producer as a multifaceted multi-tasker. The 52-week journey of a movie from script to screen, along with the business strategy that lies behind getting approval for a project—referred to as 'green-lighting'—is charted in Chapter 4. The third and final part of the book details the entrepreneurial producer and the essential nature of moviemaking juxtaposed with the stress of 'starry tantrums' and the pressure of achieving the perfect combination to harvest business potential. This is discussed in Chapter 5. Chapter 6 examines the reality of the movie business by explaining the cycle of blockbusters and disasters. The final chapter of this book provides a road map for the future of entrepreneurship in Indian cinema, with a specific focus on the entrepreneurial way ahead for Indian cinema.

Conclusion

The Indian movie industry is the largest in terms of volume, increasing in significance for the Indian economy as well as the global economy. Investigating the Indian movie industry positions it where it should be: at the forefront of our minds in the world of scholarship on the movie business and entrepreneurship. Studying the Indian independent producer can be seen as a foundation upon which a framework for the Indian movie industry can be built, thus fostering greater entrepreneurial success and reducing the failure rate of movie projects that bring loss and heartache to independent producers, their families and backers. Moviemaking is a creative business. It has entered the entrepreneurship lexicon more recently than other types of entrepreneurship. But it is just as important. Although the complexity of synthesising art and commerce persists, a robust system to encourage entrepreneurship and ensure a professional approach to moviemaking will make it less of a gamble and more of a promising entrepreneurial activity. It will usher in opportunities for recognition, team formation and resource allocation that will help build organisations that last for many generations, and plant the flag of Indian cinema into the map of world cinema. These are big claims, but the size of the Indian movie business deserves such claims to be tested, as they shall be throughout this book.

References

Central Board of Film Certification 2017, Ministry of Information and Broadcasting, Government of India. *Annual Report April 2016 to March 2017*. accessed 24/05/19, www.cbfcindia.gov.in/main/CBFC_English/Attachments/AR_2016-17_English.pdf.

Elberse, A 2013, *Blockbusters: Hit-making, Risk-taking and the Big Business of Entertainment*, Henry Holt and Co, New York.

Eliashberg, J, Elberse, A and Leenders, MAAM 2006, 'The motion pictures industry: Critical issues in practice, current research, and new research directions', *Marketing Science*, vol. 25, no. 6, pp. 638–661.

EY 2019, *A Billion Screens of Opportunity*, Report published for Federation of Indian Chamber of Commerce and Industry (FICCI), Mumbai, India.

Garg, PN and Parikh, IJ 1986, 'Managers and corporate cultures: The case of Indian organizations', *Management International Review*, vol. 26, no. 3, pp. 50–66.

Geursen, GM and Dana, LP 2001, 'International entrepreneurship: The concept of intellectual internationalisation', *Journal of Enterprising Culture*, vol. 9, no. 3, pp. 331–352.

Govil, N 2009, 'Wind (fall) from the East', *Television and New Media*, vol. 10, no. 1, pp. 63–65.

KPMG India 2017, *Media for the masses: The promise unfolds Indian media and entertainment industry report*, accessed 30/05/19, https://assets.kpmg/content/dam/kpmg/in/pdf/2017/04/FICCI-Frames-2017.pdf.

Litman, BR and Kohl, LS 1989, 'Predicting financial success of motion pictures: The 80s experience', *Journal of Media Economics*, vol. 2, pp. 35–50.

Lorenzen, M and Täube, FA 2008, 'Breakout from Bollywood? The roles of social networks and regulation in the evolution of Indian movie industry', *Journal of International Management*, vol. 14, pp. 286–299.

Motion Picture Association of America 2017, *Theme (A Comprehensive Analysis and Survey of the Theatrical and Home Entertainment Market Environment) Report*, MPAA, Washington, DC.

Prag, J and Casavant, J 1994, 'An empirical study of the determinants of revenues and marketing expenditures in the motion picture industry', *Journal of Cultural Economics*, vol. 18, pp. 217–235.

Ravid, SA 1999, 'Information blockbusters and stars: A study of the movie industry', *Journal of Business*, vol. 72, no. 4, pp. 463–492.

Roy, A and Mukherjee, K 2017, 'Entrepreneurial Education in India', *International Journal of Advanced Engineering and Management*, vol. 2, no. 1, pp. 15–20.

Sparviero, S 2015, 'Hollywood creative accounting: The success rate of major motion pictures', *Media Industries Journal*, vol. 2, pp. 19–36.

Wallace, WT, Seigerman, A and Holbrook, MB 1993, 'The role of actors and actresses in the success of movies: How much is a movie star worth?', *Journal of Cultural Economics*, vol. 17, no. 1, pp. 1–27.

PART I

Evolution of the Indian movie business

1

INDIAN MOVIE ENTREPRENEURSHIP

Opening credits

> *There are [a] large number of people in India below the poverty line; there are large numbers of people who lead a meagre existence. They want to find a little escape from the hardships of life and come and watch something colourful, exciting and musical. Indian Cinema provides that.*
>
> Amitabh Bachchan, India's superstar actor, entrepreneur

> *The India[n] movie industry [is] leading to a rise of entrepreneurs.*
>
> Ankit Kapoor, Head of Business Development and
> Operations, MovieTime Cineplex Pty Ltd

Introduction

The Indian movie industry is full of entrepreneurs who play a large part in entertainment, leisure and social life, not only in India but also globally. With three times the output of Hollywood, the Indian movie industry—comprising far more than Bollywood, as this book will demonstrate—has been successful despite the challenges of high taxes, bureaucratic complexity, multiple languages and a decentralised focus in various Indian cities and regions. It continues to increase due to the growing Indian diaspora, the rise of India as an exotic tourist destination with campaigns such as 'Incredible India', digital technologies, wide marketing strategies and the role of the producer. Indian movies are financed mainly by entrepreneurial capital (Kapoor 2018), to which producers are central. It is the entrepreneurial Indian movie producer that is the focus of this book.

The idea of writing a book on Indian movies and the entrepreneurial journey of the producer came about for both positive and negative reasons. On the positive side, some of those Indian movie producers who succeeded, failed and succeeded again have been overlooked. Preliminary online searches reveal a global interest in Indian entrepreneurs, but what they are achieving in the movie industry is less well known. Yet the Indian movie industry is booming, getting bigger and doing better on the world stage and deserves to be spruiked more widely than it is. On the negative side, after observing the Western focus on the cultural and creative industries and their management, especially in movies, it became obvious that there is a gap in knowledge about one of the largest movie industries in the world. At a time of growth in the Asian diaspora, including India, little is being written on their creative industries' development and expansion into the Western world. Indeed, in the review of the literature on movies, Eliashberg, Elberse and Leenders (2006) mention in passing that the Indian movie industry is the biggest in the world and then dismiss it, focusing instead on the US movie industry. As the biggest commercial movie cluster globally, Indian movies have huge growth for an emerging economy. Yet, largely, it is being ignored. This book demonstrates how the existence of a well-defined and geographically centred network of producers, with stakeholders such as directors, actors and audiences, can act as entrepreneurs in their moviemaking roles in India. The book looks beyond Bollywood to movie networks in all the other 'woods' in the Indian movie industry, such as Tollywood, Kollywood, Mollywood and Sandalwood (explained in detail in Chapter 2), to name a few. The book adds a new perspective to entrepreneurial theory by suggesting that, given certain networks, Indian movies, through their producers, can evolve and develop, expand and grow, not only in India but throughout the world.

As in other Asian countries, and indeed the United States, there has been a sharp rise in movie business activity in the entertainment sector. The Indian filmed entertainment sector grew by 10.6 per cent from 2017 to US$2.8 billion in 2018, with projected growth to US$3.4 billion by 2021 (EY 2019). As this strong, dynamic growth is due mostly to the movie industry, where many businesses are microenterprises and owned by independent producers, it is undisputable that the entertainment sector in India has been subject to far-reaching changes in strategy and structure. Many factors have contributed to this development. For example, government programmes have encouraged self-employment ventures; there is also a growing appreciation of entrepreneurship in India and cinema was designated a national strategic industry in 1997 (Kolluri and Lee 2016).

However, there are problems with entrepreneurship undertaken by producers in the movie industry in India. For example, there is work and income insecurity due to the uncertainty of movie success in the market, as well as difficulties with self-perception as entrepreneurs are artistic and creative people who may not appreciate the business side of their enterprise as well as they should (Hausmann 2010). Furthermore, labour markets are uncertain, with an oversupply of skilled labour and creatives as well as a need for flexibility, the amalgamation of creative ideas and commercial practices. Finally, education may not prepare movie producers for work as entrepreneurs because their courses focus on the development of creative ideas and movie process models. Indian movie producers come from a variety of backgrounds—but rarely with a business education behind them—are mostly male and take their chances in a turbulent industry.

Despite the odds being heavily stacked against them, why do entrepreneurial opportunity-seekers venture as producers into the domain of movie production? How do entrepreneurial producers cope with the spectre of failure that continuously haunts them? What drives them to be proactive in producing movies, time and time again, despite the risks and innovations required? Are they in it just for money or fame, or for something bigger? These are the questions that we consider in this book. One of the most successful producers in the history of cinema, George Lucas, labelled movie production as a terribly painful experience despite it also being labelled as leading to the rise of entrepreneurs. Even after attaining fame and amassing a fortune, why does Lucas call it a painful experience? There is no one-word answer to this question. Responses like 'passion' and 'creativity' can only answer part of the question. This book will examine entrepreneurial producer experiences and the opportunities they create in order to better understand Indian movies as a phenomenon.

In this book, we examine the rapidly growing and expanding Indian movie industry from an entrepreneurial perspective, using the producer as our primary source of information. We do this for three reasons. First and foremost, there is a need to balance the scorecard on movies so that we consider the Indian subcontinent, which has largely been ignored to date. We intend to share insights into the movie industry and its functionaries in order to stimulate research that is relevant to managers and scholars in policy, praxis, arts, entertainment and beyond. Next, we are convinced that industry-specific research can benefit the social sciences; we intend our study to prompt others to examine markets outside the USA, where there is a burgeoning activity that affects the world. We focus on Indian movies and divide our attention into three sections. First, the different strands of Indian movies. Second, the script-to-screen journey over 52 weeks. Finally, the key players in the journey to the box office and audiences enjoying the movie: producers, cast, crew, financiers and exhibitors. This three-part journey is framed by our examination of the entrepreneurial producer.

Indian movie industry ecosystem

In the movie ecosystem, there are major studios in India, independent producers and distributors, national and regional exhibitors and art houses. Studios typically engage in movie financing, movie production, movie distribution, movie promotion and advertising. This is not much different from the USA's movie industry (Eliashberg, Elberse and Leenders 2006). Here, we consider the entrepreneurial producer in the ecosystem, but it is beyond the scope of this book to examine Indian movie distribution and production, except in passing, or indeed audiences—a study which has a long history, not only in Western movies but also in Indian movies. We focus on the Indian movie producer and consider their role in the production process (see Figure 1.1).

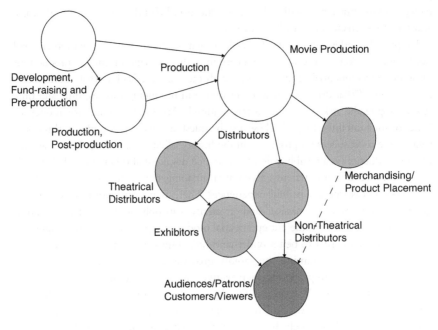

1.1 Movie industry production process

Definitions

Entrepreneurship

Entrepreneurship is defined as the discovery, evaluation and exploitation of future services and goods in which the entrepreneur makes creative decisions in order to construct the means and/or the ends of something new. It consists of three central underlying dimensions that are exploited by entrepreneurial individuals in order to harness opportunities: innovation, risk-taking and pro-activeness. Innovation relates to how the entrepreneur searches for new opportunities. Successful innovation is located in the marketplace of ideas. Risk-taking relates to how innovation is embedded in the organisation, society or community but also to the willingness of individuals to commit significant resources to opportunities. Pro-activeness concerns making things happen through perseverance and adaptability and by doing things differently. It exists before, during and after the lifetime of a particular business since it is partly shaped by the social world and by the individual decision maker (Fillis and Rentschler 2006). An entrepreneur tends to make decisions which are partly influenced by the organisation's resources, but which are ultimately made, irrespective of these resources, through the process of intuition. In this book, the entrepreneur examined is the movie producer. However, the success of the creative ideas generated by innovative behaviour and risk-taking is influenced by the ecosystem or the factors in the environment that contribute to success or failure. In this book, we place the entrepreneurial producer in the ecosystem as they make creative decisions, take risks, behave pro-actively and innovate.

Entrepreneurship in the cultural and creative industries has mostly been addressed from a business start-up perspective (e.g., Hausmann 2010; Preece 2011) rather than being examined from the point of view of an established business (Rusak 2016). The salient dimensions of entrepreneurship have been identified as innovation, risk-taking and pro-activeness, with two additional constructs added, being aggressiveness and autonomy (Lumpkin and Dess 1996). Aggressiveness is understood to entail the intensity of organisational efforts to outperform rivals in a strongly offensive posture in response to threats. Autonomy refers to new venture creation, which individual and team-based entrepreneurs bring to fruition. Following Rusak (2016), the latter two dimensions are not examined as they are deemed to be less appropriate to the cultural and creative industries.

Producer

A producer is the person who entrepreneurially develops a movie through a succession of creative decisions, absorbing the risk and economic implications. Each movie is unique and a new venture. However, in general in Indian movies, they entail a story of love, happiness and success in life and work, based on stereotypical and mythical, but idealised, stories. This book focuses on the producer who oversees the production process.

Once the movie has been made, it needs to be distributed to a network of cinemas and released to the market via cinema networks. It entails a wide range of marketing decisions encompassing movie release dates, screens on which to show the movie, and advertising media to promote the movie. A key indicator of success in distribution is box office takings, or ticket sales, and income obtained from them. It is important as it provides a baseline for determining whether the movie will be released in ancillary formats such as DVD or online streaming. A movie that grosses US$100 million was traditionally considered a blockbuster, i.e., a movie that is so popular with the movie-going public that it has exceeded all normal parameters in sales. Movie distribution success is aided by enabling movies to be screened in single-screen cinemas and in complexes (multiplexes with 8 to 15 screens and megaplexes with more than 16 screens). It does not include viewing movies on iPhones, watching movies on the internet or playing video games, all of which are threats to the movie exhibition business. While distribution and exhibition are outside the focus of this book, they will be mentioned in passing as they are, of course, important to the success of a movie and of the role of the entrepreneurial producer in obtaining opportunities for such success.

Entrepreneurial dimensions of the Indian movie industry

What has been achieved in the Indian movie industry can be explained partly by a developing economy moving from knowledge-based activities to creativity, innovation, entrepreneurship and imagination (Van Den Broeck, Cools and Maenhout 2008; Oke, Munshi and Walumbwa 2009). Entrepreneurship can be defined as the process of creating value for business and social communities by bringing together unique combinations of public and private resources to exploit economic, social or cultural opportunities in an environment of change (Fillis and Rentschler 2010). Entrepreneurship consists of three central underlying dimensions: innovation, risk-taking and pro-activeness. Innovation relates to how the entrepreneur searches for new opportunities. In movies, innovation refers to new stories, new actors and creative use of the digital world to advance the evolution of movie industry practice. Digital developments are integral to innovation in movies and drive change for production, distribution, exhibition and audiences.

Successful innovation is again located in the marketplace of ideas. Risk-taking relates to how innovation is embedded in the movie company, but also to the willingness of individual producers or movie studio executives to commit significant resources to opportunities—to see a movie to completion and to ensure the movie is satisfactory for the movie-going public. Pro-activeness concerns making things happen through perseverance, adaptability and by doing things differently. It exists before, during and after the lifetime of a particular movie since it is partly shaped by the social world, the organisations and conglomerates involved and by individual decision makers (Fillis and Rentschler 2006). An entrepreneur tends to make decisions which are partly influenced by the organisation's resources, but which, ultimately, are made irrespective of these resources through the process of intuition.

The producer as entrepreneur

As we seek to understand the producer as an entrepreneur, and because motivation plays such an important role in the entrepreneurial creation of creative works such as movies, creative organisations like studios and movie success in general, we provide a dynamic framework for entrepreneurial success in the movie industry (see Figure 1.2).

An entrepreneur is someone who is self-employed; one who starts up, organises, manages and assumes responsibility for a creative business that offers a personal challenge to create something new, innovative and risky through

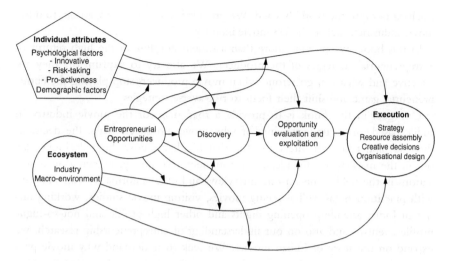

1.2 Model of the entrepreneurial process (adapted from Shane 2003)

personal pro-activeness. Producers as entrepreneurs put up their own finance or raise finance to support the creation of a movie: a risky business. Being a movie producer is bounded by uncertainty, impediments, failures and frustrations associated with bringing to fruition a new, creative concept. Not surprisingly, it is something that fascinates people. What is it that drives movie producers to take on the risk, the innovation and the independent nature of raising funds for an uncertain venture? In order to answer this question, we are interested in the content of specific things within individual movie producers that initiate, direct and sustain their drive to create a new movie. We are also interested in the dynamic processes that explain how behaviour initiates, directs and sustains the development of a new movie. Hence, while we discuss the characteristics, attitudes and beliefs of movie producers as entrepreneurs, we also go beyond them to examine contextual factors and external forces.

Conclusion

This chapter introduced the Indian movie producer against the landscape of a growing and burgeoning Indian movie industry that is less well known than it should be. It provided an overview of the Indian movie industry under the three key headings of production, movie distribution and movie exhibition, which provided a backdrop to the entrepreneurial role of the Indian movie producer in Indian movie success (and, indeed, occasional failure). While we discussed topics separately, we recognise that they are inherently interlinked. Our coverage in this chapter has reviewed Indian movies from a leadership perspective as one of the major entertainment industry revenue streams for a developing nation that is reaching out into the world beyond. We provided some brief comparisons to other movie industries, such as the US movie industry.

In this book, we provide more than a simple storyline of the high returns of entrepreneurial strategies of the producer. We also try to explain *why* they are effective and what can go wrong when movie producers stop playing the entrepreneurial game and shift their focus to risk-averse strategies.

Our goal in this book is to provide a road map for the movie industry in India, based on an understanding of why movie producers make the decisions they do, and based on interview data that highlights how those decisions play out in the marketplace for ideas, entertainment and money. Drawing on observations in the field—one-on-one interviews and other informative conversations with practitioners (as well as seeing movies, visiting movie studios, working on-site in India, attending opening nights and other high-profile and not-so-high-profile events)—and also on our understanding of entrepreneurship research, we expand on the story of Indian movies. We seek to understand why movie producers do what they do, how they do it, and what strategies they use for success (and of course why they sometimes fail).

The lessons learned in this book can be applied to television, music, book publishing and digital entertainment, to name a few sectors. We seek to provide you, the reader, with cases that resonate today but the lessons are timeless and applicable whatever the time span. If you are a movie fan, cinema-goer and watch current and past movies in binge session, you will find this book valuable, entertaining and useful for theory and praxis. There is something in it for you.

While consumer and audience behaviour is critical to the success of the Indian movie industry, we leave that to another book. Our focus is on the perspective that addresses key questions such as: what is the entrepreneurial nature of the producer that sees them succeed? How have Indian movies changed over time? What role does the producer play in interaction with other key players in the Indian movie industry? How do producers interact with movie studios and independent moviemakers? How do Indian movies finance their productions? Knowledge of these key components of Indian movie industry production, distribution and consumption will provide interest on their own but also help frame managerial and entrepreneurial issues central to this book.

References

Eliashberg, J, Elberse, A and Leenders, MAAM 2006, 'The motion pictures industry: Critical issues in practice, current research, and new research directions', *Marketing Science*, vol. 25, no. 6, pp. 638–661.

EY 2019, *A billion screens of opportunity* report published for Federation of Indian Chamber of Commerce and Industry (FICCI), Mumbai, India.

Fillis, I and Rentschler, R 2006, *Creative Marketing: An Extended Metaphor for Marketing in a New Age*, Palgrave Macmillan, Basingstoke.

Fillis, I and Rentschler, R 2010, 'The Role of Creativity in Entrepreneurship', *Journal of Enterprising Culture*, vol. 18, no. 1, pp. 49–81.

Hausmann, A 2010, 'German artists between bohemian idealism and entrepreneurial dynamics', *International Journal of Arts Management*, vol. 12, no. 2, pp. 17–29.

Kapoor, A 2018, 'How the Indian movie industry is boosting entrepreneurship', *Entrepreneur*, 18 January, www.entrepreneur.com/article/307667.

Kolluri, S and Lee, TH 2016, 'Situating Hong Kong and Bollywood cinemas in the global', in TH Lee and S Kolluri (eds), *Kong Hong and Bollywood: Globalization of Asian Cinema*, pp. 1–25, Palgrave Macmillan, New York.

Lumpkin, GT and Dess, GG 1996, 'Clarifying the entrepreneurial orientation construct and linking it to performance', *Academy of Management Review*, vol. 21, no. 1, pp. 135–172.

Oke, A, Munshi, N and Walumbwa, FO 2009, 'The influence of leadership on innovation processes and activities', *Organizational Dynamics*, vol. 38, no. 1, pp. 64–72.

Preece, S 2011, 'Performing arts entrepreneurship: Toward a research agenda Australia', *The Journal of Arts Management, Law and Society*, vol. 41, no. 2, pp. 103–120.

Rusak, H 2016, 'Corporate entrepreneurship in the arts in Western Australia', *The Journal of Arts Management, Law and Society*, vol. 46, no. 4, pp. 153–163.

Shane, S 2003, *A General Theory of Entrepreneurship: The Individual—Opportunity Nexus*, Edward Elgar, Cheltenham.

Van Den Broeck, H, Cools, E and Maenhout, T 2008, 'A case study of art economy– Building bridges between art and enterprise: Belgian businesses stimulate creativity and innovation through art', *Journal of Management and Organization*, vol. 14, pp. 573–587.

2

INDIAN MOVIE DIVERSITY

The different woods

Exactly at this location, my father used to hold discussions and make payments, he employed five individuals who went on to become Chief Ministers. That is our legacy.

AVM Saravanan, octogenarian producer and owner of one of the oldest functioning movie studios in India

Introduction

Before we can start to discuss the role of the entrepreneurial Indian movie producer in Indian movie success (and failure), it is important to map out the scope of the Indian movie business. It is vast—bigger than Hollywood and much broader and deeper than Bollywood. The impact of the opening statement at the beginning of this chapter is profound. It left a strong impression on us as we realised cinema, politics and social life in India are entwined. Cinema is a way of life in India, with a footprint spanning the entire length and breadth of the nation and spilling over into neighbouring countries. Though critics tend to dismiss Indian cinema as largely escapist fare (Dickey 1995), it is precisely this escapism that spawned an industry that has survived for more than a century and evolved into South Asia's cheapest form of entertainment. One of the few benefits of British colonisation was India's use of English as a national language, thereby opening avenues to appreciate the cinema of Britain in its heyday. During the British era, from the 19th to 20th centuries, Indian moviemakers had access to equipment and technology from Britain, which was quickly adapted to the local conditions and commercial costs. Against this backdrop, in 1913, *Raja Harishchandra* was conceived and launched as the first Indian movie by Dhundiraj Govind Phalke—popularly known as Dada Saheb Phalke (Ganti 2013, p. 8). Phalke, who was based in Bombay, is credited with creating India's first full-length feature movie and thereby earned the title of the Father of Indian Cinema.

Following Phalke's lead, other enterprising individuals ventured into the business of cinema sporadically till the 1940s. After the end of the Second World War and the independence of India in 1947, the Indian movie industry started spreading in different directions—both in terms of geography and genre/subject—of the country. In 1932, *American Cinematographer*, for the first time (Prasad 2003) and obviously as a portmanteau word to accompany Hollywood, used the word 'Tollywood' to refer to the Bengali movie industry, based in the Tollygunge area of Calcutta. Since that point in history, the 'wood' portmanteau has stuck.

For the past 123 years, ever since the Lumiere brothers made the first movie in 1896, the movie industry has typically operated in geographical ecosystems (see Figure 2.1). Though there might be several reasons behind the formation of these ecosystems, the most important reasons are: availability of land, accessibility, infrastructure and the pooling of talent. The major ecosystems that come to mind are Hollywood (named after the holly plants growing in California); the Indian movie industry; the European movie industry (encompassing French, British, Italian, German, Russian and other smaller industries); Hong Kong (now increasingly overshadowed by Shanghai, China) and Nigeria; and African Cinema. Hollywood is synonymous with the North American style of moviemaking, and it was historically located in a suburb called Hollywood in Los Angeles County in the USA. Though Hollywood is the most popular movie industry in the world, it is by no means the largest in terms of volume. That credit goes to the Indian movie industry (CBFC 2017). Referring to Indian cinema as 'Bollywood' is akin to calling the whole of British cinema, French cinema, Italian cinema and German cinema as 'Eurowood'. Apart from doing serious disservice to these vibrant industries, it is a lazy way of measuring cinema against the Hollywood barometer. Though the exact origin of the word Bollywood is not clear—with several claiming the honour of the coinage—it is nonetheless a misnomer for Indian cinema. Bombay/Mumbai is not the largest producer of Indian movies, as Madras/Chennai (poorly labelled 'Kollywood' because of its location in Kodambakam) and Hyderabad (again, sadly labelled as Tollywood because of the Telugu-language movies produced) in the South produce more movies annually. However, popular perception, largely disseminated by the international as well as the Indian press, does seem to have imprinted the name Bollywood.

The fascination with the suffix 'wood' seems to be unstoppable. The Malayalam movie industry of Kerala based in Kochi is referred to as 'Mollywood' and the Kannada movie industry of Karnataka, based in Bangalore, is called 'Sandalwood', because of the actual wood grown extensively in that state. In terms of geographic reasoning, Sandalwood comes closest to Hollywood. All these 'woods' tend to achieve is to illustrate the fact that there are several movie industries thriving in India under one large umbrella called the Indian movie industry. Though the Indian movie industry can trace its origins to 1913, there were several historical events that shaped the course of its evolution. The period 1913–1947 is distinct because of the fact that India was a colony of the British, whose influence is visible,

2.1 Indian movie regions

be it in the style of moviemaking or due to the severe restrictions and censorship conditions imposed. For the British, it was important that India remain a commercial market for cinema produced locally and encouraging indigenous talent was not a priority. Additionally, the British establishment was concerned that cinema would be used as a propaganda vehicle for inciting nationalistic passion and demanding freedom from British rule. These concerns ensured world cinema did not find its way onto Indian screens while, at the same time, guaranteed any content even remotely anti-British was forbidden to be screened.

Creative art evolves from society and sanctions that are placed on it. Indian cinema during British rule evolved to be a mere extension of theatre and drama. In fact, if we were to view the movies of that era, we would not be blamed for assuming the content on our screen was a video recording of some play or theatre show. This was partly due to the lack of expertise and partly due to the fear of restrictions and censoring by the British administration. Mythology and folklore were considered safe bets because they did not incur the wrath of the administration; additionally, the audience could relate to the stories, and were in awe of the technology of the motion picture (Baskaran 2009). It is against this backdrop that we see the movies of the era of British colonial rule relying heavily on the stories and fables from the holy books of Hinduism. Another crucial aspect that needs to be noted during this era was the demarcation of India into administrative regions by the British. Initially, the British East India Company, then the British Empire, operated from Calcutta, which was its capital from 1722 to 1911. However, being in the eastern part of the country, it was not very conducive for administration, resulting in the capital shifting to Delhi (Dalrymple 2019).

Calcutta is on the eastern side of India; the British set it up as a port for trade due to its geographic convenience. Bombay was established as a port on the western side and Madras as a port on the southern side of India. It is no coincidence that the bulk of India's movie industry operates from these three cities even today. By virtue of being port cities, they established themselves as centres of trade, thereby attracting artists, intellectuals, entrepreneurs and people seeking to make a living. The location of Delhi, a landlocked city, as an administrative capital attracted a different profile of citizenry, and cinema in particular, and arts in general, did not take root. Calcutta, Bombay and Madras attracted the maximum number of foreign visitors during the British era, mainly due to the convenience of travel, but also due to these three states offering a window into the culture of that particular region of India. The Bengali movie industry was born in Calcutta, then referred to as the Bengal Presidency, and today caters to the Bengali-speaking population—not only in India but also in Bangladesh. In a south Calcutta suburb called Tollygunge, named after Colonel William Tolly, the Bengali movie industry was born, and so was the name Tollywood (Prasad 2003). The Marathi and Hindi movie industries were born in the western city of Bombay—then referred to as the Bombay and Sind Presidency—they operate from that city to the present day even since Sind became part of Pakistan. The name Bollywood comes from this association with Bombay. Hindi was designated as the national language of India along with English. This unofficially made Hindi-language cinema the national cinema of India, thereby creating the mistaken notion that Bollywood is representative of the Indian movie industry.

The Tamil, Telugu, Malayalam and Kannada movie industries were all born in Madras because there were no separate states for these languages, and they were all part of the Madras Presidency. Kodambakam, a western suburb of Madras, was the centre of all the moviemaking activities for these four languages. Therefore, the portmanteau word of Kollywood was bestowed upon it. In fact, until the late 1980s, all these four language movies were being produced in Madras. It was during the late 1980s and early 1990s that the four languages decided to move to their respective states and establish separate identities. This move gave rise to the portmanteaus of Mollywood, Sandalwood and Tollywood, as mentioned earlier. Though the number of movies produced in Madras has decreased now, for close to 40 years following Indian independence in 1947, it was the epicentre of all movie activities in South India, resulting in Madras producing more movies annually than Hollywood (Guy 2016).

After India gained independence from the British, the scale, tone and tenor of movie production underwent a massive transformation. Even though the cities of Calcutta, Bombay and Madras changed their names to the pre-British-era names of Kolkata, Mumbai and Chennai respectively, their status as the most prominent movie centres in India did not change. Shortly before Indian independence, the Second World War ended, bringing home many Indians who had travelled to Malaya (now Malaysia and Singapore), Burma (now Myanmar) and Ceylon (now Sri Lanka) for their livelihoods and business opportunities. Many of them returned with fortunes they had made and they invested into the Indian movie industry, either directly setting up movie studios and movie production houses, or by financing movie ventures. This, in a way, can be termed the second wave of movie entrepreneurs coinciding with the migrants who moved back after India was partitioned into India and Pakistan. From 1947 to the present day, Indian cinema has moved forward in tune with the times. From the late 1940s to the late 1960s, Indian cinema balanced entertainment and social relevance with topics ranging from women's empowerment, a classless society and progressive thinking. Though there are smaller industries operating in Punjab, Assam, Orissa and central India, the volume of movies and the scale of production in these industries is much smaller compared to the industries operating out of Mumbai, Chennai and Kolkata.

Bengali movie industry

Due to the significance of being a capital city of the British Empire in its peak, and being home to a large population with Hindu Bengali, Muslim Bengali and Gurkha ethnicity, Calcutta enjoyed a pre-eminent position in the cultural landscape of India. Citizens of Calcutta were looked upon with awe and admiration for their intellect, education and literary strength. Geographically located on the eastern side of India, Calcutta was not only a window into Bengali culture but also closest to the influence of China. It is no surprise that one of the most violent and aggressive manifestations of communist philosophy originated from a small village called Naxalbari (Chowdhury 2018), close to present day Bangladesh and near the hills of Darjeeling. Chairman Mao's principles were the guiding doctrines for the founders of the Naxalbari movement, which advocates a classless society. The followers of this movement, labelled as Maoists, carried out insurgency activities against the Indian government. Needless to say, there were many writers and thinkers who believed in this ideology and espoused the cause of communist philosophy. The impact of this thinking was visible in the cinema of Calcutta. For 34 years, a democratically elected communist government was in power in the state of West Bengal, with Calcutta as its capital. In a way, Bengali cinema, with its realistic portrayal of characters and situations, does not fit into the 'singing and dancing' image of Indian cinema.

Rabindranath Tagore, the Nobel Prize-winning poet from Bengal, established his Santi Niketan (abode of peace) school, which grew into a formidable university, near Calcutta. A majority of the creative artists in Bengal claim their affiliation with Tagore's style of borderless education that is in harmony with nature and the Indian ethos. Arguably one of the internationally best-known Indian directors is Satyajit Ray, an alumnus of Tagore's university. Ray was honoured with a lifetime achievement award by the Academy of Motion Pictures, Arts and Sciences. Ray's ability as an extraordinary moviemaker was established with his globally acclaimed trilogy of *Apu* movies, recognised and feted across the world for its coming-of-age theme. *Song of the Little Road*, *Unvanquished*, and the *World of Apu* are the three titles in this trilogy, dealing with the childhood, education, maturity and adulthood of its central character Apu. Ray was a pioneer in Bengali cinema, forging a pathway for many aspiring and creative directors, such as Ritwik Ghatak, Mrinal Sen and Aparna Sen, to pursue their dreams and craft meaningful stories on celluloid.

The distinguishing feature of the Bengali movie industry is its success in maintaining a perfect balance between the commercial demands of the box office and the artistic pursuit of cinema as an art. As we note in the later sections of this chapter, few movie industries in India were able to resist the allure of commercialisation and a formula-driven approach. Whether Bengali society itself values the superiority of intellect over financial gain is a moot point. The reality is that the Bengali movie industry does not stick to a stereotypical escapist plot, with lavishly mounted song-and-dance sequences unconnected to the main narrative but added for sheer entertainment value. This distinguishing feature sets the Bengali movie industry apart from its equivalents.

Hindi movie industry

As mentioned earlier, Bombay/Mumbai was established as the commercial capital of India, and it was home to the largest business houses as well as movie studios. Though the local language was Marathi, Hindi was accepted as the language of business as well as the national language, resulting in both the Marathi and the Hindi movie industries operating from Mumbai. Early pioneers in cinema, like Dada Phalke, doubling up as both the producer and director— and in many instances, the leading man also—relied on the mythological genre to provide them with content. The first Indian movie, *Raja Harishchandra*, is a silent movie by Phalke and it narrates the story of a virtuous king (Chabria, Usai, and Virchand 1994), who does not lie even when facing the death of his son and wife. Though this movie launched Indian cinema, it was not until 1930, when *Alam Ara*, the first Indian movie with sound, was released by Ardeshir Irani, that the Indian movie industry started carving a niche for itself. Both the producers and audience realised the exciting possibility of incorporating sound into a motion picture rather than the tiring narration of a translator who positioned himself at the corner of the screen and yelled like a herald. Most producers at this stage were conservative and relied on themes that were safe, both from the perspective of audience reception and the risk of alienating the British censors.

After the partition of India, a new wave of immigrants arrived in Bombay and they brought their life experiences into cinema. The traditional and established production houses like the Prabhat Movie Company and V Shantaram's Rajkamal Kala Mandir had to wind up and give way to the new generation of producers like Raj Kapoor's RK studios, BR Chopra, Yash Chopra, GN Sippy and Barjatya's Rajshree Productions. Human relationships and the struggle to establish oneself in the new order were recurring central themes in most of the movies during this timeframe. Though there was star power, it was still the producers who called the shots and functioned in a truly entrepreneurial style when scouting for opportunities and launching ventures that could tap into the potential offered by such occasions. The producers mentioned above were pioneers not only in taking Indian cinema to its next level but in exploring different genres inspired by world cinema. Vittorio De Sica's *Bicycle Thieves* and themes from Charlie Chaplin inspired many stories and leading-man characterisations in several Hindi movies. For 25 years following independence, Hindi cinema was exploring themes that showcased the struggles of the common man but ended on a note of optimism and hope for the future. Though a clear divide between the rich and poor was visible on-screen, moviemakers ensured that the audience related to the travails of the poor and to success against all the odds, thus reflecting the aspiration of a society that believed in hard work for a better life.

The 1970s brought change to Indian society and for Indian audiences. This again reflected society's angst about poor employment prospects, an almost stagnating economy with negligible growth rates and a mass exodus of the talent pool to foreign shores, resulting in anger towards the establishment. This dramatic change in audience perception is visible in the phenomenon of superstardom. India's first superstar was Rajesh Khanna (Bhatia 2012) who shone throughout the late 1960s till the early 1970s. Rajesh Khanna was a stereotypical romantic hero indulging in song-and-dance sequences with his leading lady. The central theme of his movies was romance, with love triumphing at its climax when the male lead always won over his leading lady.

Indian society retained a romantic outlook, and this resulted in Rajesh Khanna becoming a superstar, along with his trademark head movements and swagger, which became stereotypical depictions of Indian cinema. However, this phase only lasted five years. Fifteen consecutive blockbusters later, audiences started to tire of the routine and same, hackneyed themes. Producers who created this phenomenon started looking out for another concept to grab audiences' attention.

Salim Khan and Javed Akhtar—credited on-screen as Salim-Javed—created a formula loosely labelled as the angry young man; a young man angry with the system who rebels against it, taking up the cause of the underprivileged. This formula created another superstar called Amitabh Bachchan. The angst in Indian society made audiences yearn for an escapist formula that would make them forget the harsh reality of their lives and identify with the leading man who single-handedly changes the system. Though the reality is far from the fiction depicted on-screen, audiences lapped it up, and for more than a decade Bachchan was the undisputed leading star of the Hindi movie industry. The star system was built around him and producers waited for days to get a confirmation from him. In fact, only once he agreed would producers then recruit additional cast and crew. Salim-Javed kept churning out scripts that dealt with lost and found certain key themes: reunion with family, rebelling against society and romancing a rich girl who is part of a decadent society but is willing to change. Unfortunately, this trend resulted in a change of role for the producer. The producer changed from being an entrepreneur to a manager attending to the demands of the leading man. Producers no longer called the shots in terms of assembling the best cast and crew and presenting a final product that showcased the talent of this assembled team. It was the superstar who decided the director, the leading lady and a majority of the technical crew. Unfortunately, this culture still persists in some pockets of the industry and for big star vehicles, but it has declined compared to the 1970s and 1980s.

Singing, dancing and the being-removed-from-reality fare that is associated with Indian cinema in the popular perception is a stereotype that was created during this phase of Hindi cinema. Though there was a very strong 'parallel cinema' (Krishen 1991) movement that produced excellent thought-provoking and genre-defining work, Hindi cinema became trapped in an image of its own making that it could not shed. This meant that international audiences did not see any content outside this star-driven material, which presented a lopsided image of Indian cinema. Additionally, India suffered as an economy, with muddled socialist thinking and archaic taxation laws resulting in the notorious black money syndrome: the cash economy that enabled widespread tax avoidance due to the extraordinarily high tax rates during the 1970s and 1980s. Due to high tax rates—as high as 97 per cent (Rao 2000)—Indian entrepreneurs had limited choice, resulting in a parallel economy. It was common for the cast and crew to be paid in two formats: the official payment of about 10 per cent of the 'real' remuneration paid by cheque and duly taxed at the highest rate, and the unofficial payment of the remaning 90 per cent, which was paid in cash with no paper trail. These dual payments resulted in a flourishing parallel economy. Income-tax raids to claim for unaccounted money were often used as a political tool to settle scores. Due to the lack of transparency, unscrupulous members of society who made money by racketeering or extortion gravitated to the movie industry and started 'investing' in movies. Murders, actors and technicians going missing and financiers buckling under mafia pressure were regular news items. Those were the dark days for movie entrepreneurship in the Hindi movie industry.

Closely following glasnost and perestroika, occurring in the former Soviet Union in the 1980s, India initiated its own set of economic reforms in 1991 and unleashed massive consumer demand. The 1 per cent and 2 per cent growth rate for the economy, derogatively referred to as the Hindu rate of growth (Nayar 2006), gave way to an 8 per cent average annual growth, and India started matching strides with China in economic growth, with the added benefit of a vibrant democracy. This change in the economy naturally resulted in a change in outlook for the movie industry, which also opened up avenues for corporatisation and the entry of Hollywood studios. It is common for movie industry analysts to say that the industry has cleaned up its act. Inordinate delays in shooting and lack of clarity in the release schedule of movies have become things of the past. Today, the Hindi movie industry sticks to almost-perfect production and release schedules. Once transparency and professionalism took root in the industry, it was only natural that global corporations entered the Hindi movie industry.

20th Century Fox, Disney and Viacom commissioned projects and donned the role of fully fledged Indian movie production houses, initially commencing with the Hindi movie industry and then venturing into the South: especially Tamil and Telugu movies. Fox, which was a part of media mogul Rupert Murdoch's News Corporation—recently acquired by Disney—operates as the movie production arm of the corporation, while the Star network operates as the TV and streaming content arm. In fact, all three corporations have a significant presence in both the movie and television media. In the past decade, entrepreneurial movie producers have made a strong comeback into the Hindi movie industry and they are coming up with exciting genre-bending content. The Hindi movie industry today bears a strong resemblance to Hollywood, with large corporations, large production houses, independent producers and star-driven productions all co-existing and striving to improve the overall quality of content.

Tamil movie industry

Screen life and real life tends to blur in the South of India, and this is evident from the fact that in the period from 1967 to 2016, every Chief Minister of Tamil Nadu (Tamil state) came from the movie industry, whether a former male or female actor, scriptwriter, dialogue writer or director. This trend was repeated in neighbouring Andhra Pradesh, where the Telugu movie industry is located, and where a leading male actor from the movie industry was the Chief Minister for almost a decade. Though these two states are not unique for movie stars entering politics and occupying prominent political positions, Tamil Nadu is an exception for the longevity of movie personalities occupying political positions. Nowhere else in the world did this phenomenon last uninterrupted for half a century. President Reagan and Governor Schwarzenegger in the USA and Prime Minister Estrada in the Philippines were all former actors, yet none experienced such longevity in office. To trace the reasons for this unique situation, we need to step back into history.

As discussed earlier in this chapter, the Madras Presidency was the southern port and base for British India—a rather large terrain covering six states and two union territories. Madras, as the capital of this administrative Presidency, housed the movie industries catering to the Telugu, Kannada and Malayalam languages apart from the Tamil language (Dickey 1993, 1995). Irrespective of the language spoken, all South Indians were lumped into a group referred to as Madarasis, given that they resided in the Madras Presidency. The economy in this region was primarily agrarian, and due to the cyclical nature of agriculture, especially crop harvests, the residents of the Madras Presidency experienced a very busy crop season and a relatively quiet period where agricultural activity was at its lowest. This cyclical nature had a significant impact on the cultural and cinematic landscape of the Madras Presidency, mainly due to the fact that, initially, a majority of producers were from an agricultural background and relied on farm income to finance their cinema ventures. By housing the movie industries of four main languages—Tamil, Telugu, Kannada and Malayalam— Madras evolved into a powerhouse, or engine room, for the Indian movie industry. The output was prolific and catered to an audience of all the South Indian languages, ensuring that a vibrant industry was established in Madras.

Madras was the epicentre of movie production for the four South Indian languages until the 1980s, when, due to political and logistical reasons, the Telugu movie industry shifted to Hyderabad; the Malayalam movie industry shifted to Kochi; and the Kannada movie industry shifted to Bengaluru. This section deals with the Tamil movie industry and subsequent sections present the other three industries. Tamil-speaking Indians were largely confined to the state in the most southerly part of India, Tamil Nadu. Due to plantation-worker migration (Guy 2016) and even indentured labour, there is a large Tamil-speaking population in Sri Lanka, Malaysia and Singapore and these three countries offer significant revenue potential for Tamil movies. Pioneers in the Tamil movie industry originated from either the farming or money-lending communities with established business connections in places like Rangoon (before WWII), Ceylon and Malaya.

Tamil-language cinema embraced progressive thinking and revolutionary ideology that challenged established conventions. This thinking was also aided by the fact that established rigidity in the caste system of India was challenged by the Tamil population immediately after Indian independence. This gave rise to writers, producers, directors and artists who broke mould and set up new cinematic conventions. Writers with progressive ideas developed scripts and content that challenged the status quo, and they found receptive audiences who were eager to patronise path-breaking content. The presence of an entrenched theatre circuit and culture ensured there was a good test market for content before it could be crafted into a movie script. Theatre presented an opportunity for the writers to try out new content. The audience response in one show enabled them to fine-tune or edit content in response to feedback and further refine it for launching on a larger scale for cinema. Theatre companies had wealthy landlords and members of the erstwhile royal families as their financial patrons and sponsors (Baskaran 1981). Though individual entrepreneurs set up their own theatre companies, they did not survive for long if not supported by wealthy sponsors. The risk for a theatre company was smaller compared to a movie production company, mainly due to the scale of investment. Against this backdrop, three studios and their owners were largely responsible for laying the foundations for a vibrant cinema industry in Madras.

SS Vasan of Gemini Studios was labelled the Cecil B De Mille of Indian cinema (Ashokamithran 2002). Though such high praise always suffers from subjective interpretation, in this case, it is no exaggeration. Vasan dreamed big, and he had the conviction to pursue his dreams. Starting his career as a journalist, writer and the publisher of *Ananda Vikatan* (one of the largest circulated magazines in India currently), Vasan initially branched out by shooting his own script and inadvertently commencing his production career, which spanned almost three decades. Gemini Studios, under the stewardship of Vasan, evolved into a prolific production house with multilingual movies and lavish production values. Vasan was touted as a pioneer for production design and studio management, striding like a colossus across the movies and public domains. SS Vasan was a member of the upper house of the Indian Parliament and his commitment to the cause of cinema was evident from his championing its cause to be awarded industry status—a status that yielded benefits to all employees and stakeholders. Vasan was also a founding member of the South Indian Film Chamber of Commerce, Producers Guild of India and Movie Federation of India. Playing an instrumental role in streamlining the activities of the movie industry, Vasan ensured that cinema entered the mainstream of social and political consciousness rather than being sidelined. *Chandralekha*, a movie produced and directed by Vasan, stands as one of the historic milestones in Indian cinema; the sheer grandeur and huge narrative span of this classic solidified the credentials of SS Vasan in the history of Indian cinema. Despite his successful stint as a producer, director and publisher, Vasan's major shortcoming was his failure to visualise and plan for the future and ensure that Gemini Studios survived after his death. Unfortunately, due to poor succession planning and lack of professional vision, Gemini Studios closed within a decade of Vasan's death, ending one of the illustrious chapters in Indian cinema.

AVM studios is synonymous with content that is thought-provoking as well as family-friendly. Avichi Meiyappa Chettiar was a contemporary of Vasan, and he set up the AVM studios in Madras. AVM is one of the oldest—if not the oldest— functioning studio in India, with the fourth generation now at the helm of production. The sheer volume of work produced by AVM studios reflects its lasting legacy and contribution to Indian cinema (Meiyappan 2015). Coming from a family of money lenders and financiers, Chettiar (usually referred to as AVM) had the uncanny ability to keep a tight rein on the budget of his productions, thereby ensuring that every movie made a profit. Apart from budgetary control, AVM had a creative eye that enabled him to keep a finger on the pulse of the audience, catering to popular taste and maintaining box office success. Though AVM as a production house has slowed down considerably from its heyday of producing more than 170 movies in Tamil, Telugu, Kannada, Malayalam and Hindi languages, it is a fully functional studio that possesses shooting lots and recording theatres. *Parasakthi* is one of the landmark movies from AVM, and it is no exaggeration to say this movie laid the foundation for the intense political and social upheaval that occurred in Tamil Nadu and resulted in the five-decade intrinsic link between the worlds of politics and movies. The indelible impression that AVM left on the Indian movie industry is reflected in the five Chief Ministers who once worked there, along with its legacy of introducing superstars or propelling stars to superstardom in five languages across Indian cinema. Today, AVM is making forays into new content-development avenues like web series for streaming services. With a younger generation at the helm, AVM still continues to be a major contributor to Indian cinema legacy.

Nagi Reddy and Chakrapani's friendship is legendary, and in the movie industry they were mentioned in the same breath as if they were one individual with two bodies. Nagi Reddy and Chakrapani were friends first, and partners second. In point of fact, Chakrapani was a widower and his children were raised by Nagi Reddy's wife along with her own children (Reddi 2013). Vijaya Productions was started by the two men as a movie production company that visualised the creativity of Chakrapani, who was skilled in writing and translating. Nagi Reddy provided the financial acumen in the partnership. They acquired Vauhini studios when the opportunity arose and commenced production under the banner of Vijaya Vauhini Studios. Although physically located just a stone's throw away from AVM, Vijaya Vauhini Studios focused more on Telugu-language movies, though they produced Tamil and Kannada movies too. Additionally, Vijaya Vauhini was a force to reckon with in the children's magazine sector, publishing a popular periodical in 11 different languages. Vijaya Vauhini did not take up political causes but tended to focus on entertainment with a tilt towards religious and mythological stories. *Maya Bazaar* (*Magic Market*), one of the all-time classics in the Indian movie industry, was produced by Vijaya Vauhini, and the sheer technical excellence, histrionic style, melodious music and gripping screenplay mesmerised audiences in both

Tamil and Telugu, ensuring that it stays at the top of must-watch lists. Unlike Gemini Studios, Vijaya Vauhini managed to survive, albeit in a diminished form. The actual studios have ceased operations, but the production house still produces movies sporadically, with Nagi Reddy's son and grandchildren at the helm. Chakrapani's family is no longer active. Similar to the schools and charities started by AVM, Vijaya Vauhini established hospitals and shopping malls. Though Nagi Reddy had a very public profile and served as the President of the South Indian Film Chamber of Commerce for two terms, the next generation has not been able to keep pace with the technological changes (Saraswathi 2013) that are needed to sustain the studio in the modern day.

Gemini, AVM and Vijaya Vauhini can be termed the three strong pillars of the South Indian movie industry in general, and the Tamil movie industry in particular. The work ethic and control exerted by these production houses spawned as many as 30 studios within a geographic radius of six kilometres. Unfortunately, all of these studios have now closed and the new generation of producers operate with a different work ethic and commercial sensibility. Similar to the Hindi movie industry, the advent of star culture has relegated the role of a producer from an entrepreneur to an assembler: the stars dictate the terms and the producers adhere to them. This did not augur well for production houses like Gemini, AVM and Vijaya Vauhini which had streamlined production process where the stars were part of the process rather than circumventing it. Though all the superstars of the Tamil movie industry worked with these leading production houses—in fact, they gained their superstardom because of these production houses—they did not want to relinquish their newfound authority in favour of the older system. There are a few producers who try to balance it out by producing some movies with established stars, catering to their image and demands, while at the same time making movies with new talent, thereby striving to retain their creative and financial independence. Both Disney and Fox made inroads into the Tamil movie industry. They did not entrench themselves in the system and were content to indulge in sporadic activity as they attempted to come to grips with reality on the ground. In the past decade, a noticeable change is visible in the Tamil movie industry, with younger directors opting out of the star-driven formula and focusing on content-driven movies. If the content is well made and interesting, there is a receptive audience. However, this is only a small percentage and the Tamil movie industry is at a crisis point with revenues not justifying expenditure and the market size shrinking. The percentage of successes has fallen significantly, and the number of screens available to showcase content has shrunk in comparison with other states (Cain 2015). Leading star remuneration is not commensurate with market size, which exposes producers to the rather tragic reality of a movie being classified as a blockbuster while the producer ends up making significant losses. Digital avenues have opened up new possibilities for content creation, but as long as the main source of revenue is theatrical exhibition, which continues to underperform, the crisis will remain. It is disheartening to see the tragic downslide of an industry that has spawned three other industries and was a movement at the forefront of global cinema..

Telugu movie industry

The Telugu movie industry has two phases in its evolution. The first phase was during its stint in Madras; the second phase was after its shift to Hyderabad. Though the creative output was on a par with Tamil during the forty-year period from 1947 to 1987, it was always under the shadow of the Tamil movie industry—more so after the splitting up of the Madras Presidency into different states on a linguistic basis. The states of Andhra Pradesh, with its Telugu-speaking population; Karnataka, with its Kannada-speaking population; and Kerala, with its Malayalam-speaking population came into existence in the late 1950s. This invariably led to a demand for the local movie industries to shift into their respective states. Though the shift was gradual, it did happen over a span of three decades. Initially, the producers were reluctant to shift, citing the lack of infrastructure and absence of an ecosystem as major reasons. The governments in respective states offered incentives and subsidies to encourage the local industry to shift and, with leading stars on board, the shift gained momentum. In fact, the leading stars of all three industries seized the initiative and set up their own production houses and studios in their respective states; plus they imposed a condition that their movies had to be shot in the new state. This was the nudge that the industry needed, and it resulted in en masse migration by industries. This migration drastically undercut the clout of Madras as a movie production hub, with the number of movies produced per year falling to less than 200, as opposed to its potential for producing 600 to 700 movies per year.

It is debatable whether the quality of content improved after the Telugu movie industry migrated to Hyderabad, but it helped in developing the infrastructure and creating a base from which the industry could evolve and grow. Ramoji Movie City (RFC) on the outskirts of Hyderabad, now in the newly carved-out state of Telangana, is a case in point (Nathan 2018). Modelled along the lines of large Hollywood studios, RFC is a one-stop shop for making movies—every production, post-production and ancillary facility is available and industry insiders quip that you can walk into RFC with your funds and come out with a completed movie in your hands. Such a world-class facility would not have been possible without the industry moving out from Chennai to Hyderabad. Conceived and built by a media baron with wide-ranging interests in movie production and distribution, RFC was one of the facilitators of the industry establishing itself. Long before RFC was conceived and executed, two names that are almost synonymous with the Telugu movie industry are NTR and ANR and they played a prominent role to establish the industry in Hyderabad after migrating from Madras.

Nandamuri Taraka Ramarao (NTR) strode the cinematic and political landscape of Andhra Pradesh like a titan. Acting in more than 300 movies, producing 28 and directing 16, NTR, through the sheer volume of his work, contributed to the evolution of the Telugu movie industry. In a movie career spanning four decades, NTR left his imprint on different facets of the movie industry. Though most of his movies were social dramas—mythological or religious genres were his forte and he cultivated a very loyal fan base—he managed to establish a cult status. This worked in his favour when he decided to plunge into politics at the age of 60, after taking a break from the movie world. NTR's ability to appreciate the intricacies of moviemaking, with a good handle on every craft, enabled him to mentor and build a pool of talented artists and technicians. The roots of NTR's evolution as a veritable encyclopaedia of moviemaking can be traced back largely to his stint in Madras as a paid employee in Vijaya Vauhini Studios, where he spent a considerable amount of time, and, to a lesser extent, at AVM studios. These studios presented him with an opportunity to study and master the minute aspects of moviemaking. This knowledge enabled him to become a successful producer and director. Though his foray into establishing and operating a studio was short-lived, it showcased his intentions to move the industry out of Madras and establish it in Hyderabad. Replicating the model of MGR's journey from cinema to politics in the neighbouring state, the final chapter of NTR's life concluded with him successfully launching a political party and, through meticulous canvassing, he stormed to power within nine months of establishing the party. It was estimated he travelled 100,000 kilometres (Dasu 2004)—an unparalleled feat in Indian politics—for the sake of establishing his political party. The rigorous discipline, willpower and stamina that helped to establish a successful movie career were evident in his political determination, culminating in his role as a Chief Minister.

Akkineni Nageswar Rao (ANR) was a contemporary, friend, competitor and collaborator of NTR. If NTR had an image with mass appeal, ANR had a softer image as a romantic hero, very popular with female audiences. Hailing from neighbouring villages, both ANR and NTR entered the movie industry as supporting artists, enacting minor roles and then moving onto leading roles. Though not as prolific as NTR in his output, ANR acted in close to 250 movies and continued acting almost into his final days. ANR did not direct but was a very successful producer and studio head. In fact, ANR can be credited as the pioneer of moving the movie industry from Madras to Hyderabad, as he was the earliest to establish a fully functional movie studio there. ANR was deeply influenced by his days at Vijaya Vauhini and AVM studio as a paid employee, and he used this experience as an opportunity to learn and understand the intricacies of the movie studio business. He was so involved and consumed by his passion for establishing a studio that it became his single-minded vision. This vision ensured that ANR cleared the path for establishing the Telugu movie industry in Hyderabad and led to the migration of artists and technicians from Madras to Hyderabad. Annapurna Studios, established by ANR, is one of the premier movie studios in India, managed by talented professionals and with a clear vision for the future. ANR's oft-repeated quote was, 'Cinema is our first love, and the desire to contribute to its growth is the foundation of Annapurna Studios' (annapurnastudios.com). Second- and third-generation representatives from ANR's family occupy management positions in the studios, but it is a very professional organisation that caters to the needs of the movie industry. In fact, it takes its initiative from fostering and nurturing talent in order to enhance the quality of movie professionals. Annapurna Studios established Annapurna Movie and Media School and was instrumental in building a professional culture that has created a lasting legacy.

Though there are many other contributors to the success of the Telugu movie industry, NTR and ANR can be credited as the pioneers who were instrumental in ensuring that the industry took roots and established itself. Unlike the neighbouring Tamil and Malayalam industries, the Telugu movie industry produced a limited amount of path-breaking content. Though *Maya Bazaar* (*Magic Market*) and *Sankarabharanam* (*Gods Jewel*) were path-breaking movies, both were made in Madras. Telugu movie producers were entrepreneurial in creating the medium as a commercial vehicle for the recognition and exploitation of opportunities. However, the strong social messages propagated by the Tamil and Malayalam industry were not evident in the Telugu movie industry, with occasional movies by the late T Krishna being exceptions. The Telugu movie industry operated in the mainstream commercial format and catered to the demands of an audience that craved cinema as pure entertainment. This is reflected in the largest concentration of movie screens per square kilometre being found in the Telugu movie industry. Large-scale migration of Telugu-speaking citizens to the USA since the 1970s to the present day has resulted in the North American market becoming the most lucrative overseas territory for Telugu movies (Murthy 2017). Director Rajamouli, with his two-part *Baahubali* movie, ensured that a Telugu movie stands on top of the all-time most successful Indian movies list with a box office gross of US$350 million. Set against a fictional background, along the lines of *Lord of the Rings*, *Baahubali* showcases the creative and commercial might of the Indian movie industry. With the success of *Baahubali*, it is clear that the Telugu movie industry has well and truly evolved, cutting the umbilical cord from Madras and becoming the leading commercial powerhouse for South Indian cinema.

Malayalam movie industry

The Kerala movie industry is called the cradle of creativity in Indian cinema. The majority of leading cinematographers in Indian cinema call Kerala their home state and they perfected their craft in Malayalam-language cinema before moving on to a bigger canvas. Originally, the Malayalam movie industry commenced production during the British era in the 1920s, in Trivandrum, but due to the infrastructural advantages presented by the Madras Presidency, the industry shifted to Madras in the late 1940s when India gained its independence and operated out of Madras till the early 1980s. Similar to the Telugu movie industry, the Malayalam industry also shifted out of Madras in the 1980s and established itself predominantly in Cochin (Kochi) with a minor presence in Trivandrum (Thiruvananthapuram).

Kerala as a state is an interesting paradox in the broader cultural and political context of India. It is the only state in India to have a very high rate of literacy (Chandran 1994). With abundant natural resources and beauty, Kerala is touted as God's own country. However, the paradox comes in the fact that it is the only state in India, and maybe in the world, that has a democratically elected Marxist socialist government. In fact, historically, along with West Bengal, Kerala is the womb of communist ideology in India. Though the communists have lost power and appear to have no chance of coming back to power in West Bengal, Marxist communist philosophy is still in vogue in Kerala (Jaffe and Doshi 2017). This ideology had a strong influence on moviemakers from Kerala, resulting in a highly creative output that straddles both the commercial and art worlds, throwing up bizarre examples, like an actor who performed in a lead role with the same leading lady in 130 movies.

Prem Nazir holds the Guinness World Record for acting in the maximum number of movies—720—in a leading role. A history of Malayalam cinema is not complete without referring to Prem Nazir. Though man y of his movies had unbelievably small budgets of less than US$5000, it is a recorded fact that Prem Nazir had 39 movies released in a single calendar year (Ajithkumar 2010). This speaks volumes about his prolific work as well as the output of the industry itself. Debuting as a stage actor, Nazir went on to attain great heights as a popular romantic hero who was adept at tearjerkers and melodrama, thereby endearing himself to female audiences (in the vast majority) and commanding a loyal fan base. Towards the end of his career, Prem Nazir shifted to supporting roles, and though most of his movies in a leading role were not memorable, his supporting roles were noteworthy. When the Malayalam industry was operating from Madras, Prem Nazir had the advantage of interacting with the leading actors from all other industries there, which ensured that he had access to content and stories from many projects. It was almost an unwritten rule during the 1950s and 1960s that Tamil movies featuring MGR and Sivaji would be remade into Telugu with NTR and ANR, and in Malayalam with Prem Nazir. Due to budget constraints and the pressures of commercial viability, Malayalam movies were shot on the same sets erected for Tamil and Telugu movies. The Tamil and Telugu movies were shot during regular daytime slots, and on the same set for a much-reduced rent—an almost 60–70 per cent discount—and Malayalam movies were shot during the night. A natural consequence of this constraint was most of the content was shot indoors, on sets, with a limited budget. It is not surprising that Prem Nazir could complete 39 movies in one calendar year because the same studio was used with the same set, albeit with limited modifications and set timings. Prem Nazir was noted for his output, but the trio who took Malayalam cinema to great heights were a director who treated cinema as an art form and two leading actors who viewed their work as both art and commercial venture.

Adoor Gopalakrishnan is the most well-known and fêted director in Malayalam cinema. In contrast to Prem Nazir, in a career spanning more than five decades, Adoor has directed fewer than 30 documentaries and feature movies, placing him at the other end of the spectrum to Nazir, balancing prolific commercial output and artistic expression. Adoor is credited with ushering in a new wave of Malayalam cinema and spawning many who followed his path in using cinema as a canvas to showcase art. *Elipathayam* (*Rat Trap*) (Gopalakrishnan 1985) is a shining example of Adoor's style of moviemaking and received the Sutherland Trophy from the British Film Institute. Movies as social commentary with a strong focus on the problems of societal and human evolution juxtaposed with environmental concerns are recurring themes of Adoor's movies. He is an example of how the interpretation of cinema varies according to the interpreter. With Adoor holding the fort for the artistic element of Malayalam cinema and Prem Nazir exploiting its commercial side, two leading actors gradually made their presence felt and linked the two worlds of Malayalam cinema. Mohanlal and Mammootty were at ease essaying the roles of commercial blockbuster heroes, as well as actors with unparalleled dramatic ability.

Mohanlal appeared in more than 300 movies, and versatility is his forte. An ability to get into the skin of the character and breathe life through his acting elevated Mohanlal to superstar status, in demand in Tamil, Telugu and also Malayalam (thecompleteactor.com). It might be difficult to categorise Mohanlal as a specific genre actor, but his ability to tackle roles that connected with the masses and made them identify with his characters made him an ideal star for blockbuster ventures and commercial potboilers. His ability to portray characters with a strong comic touch endeared Mohanlal to family audiences and turned him into a much sought-after leading actor. Mohanlal is an active producer of movies under his own company as well as jointly with a production company owned by his manager. As a producer, Mohanlal has gained a reputation for coming up with out-of-the-box content that connects both the commercial and the artistic aspects of cinema. His son Pranav also recently made his debut in a leading role. Mohanlal's family can certainly be called a cinema family, given that his father-in-law is a leading producer in Tamil, and his brother-in-law also continues to produce.

Mammootty appeared in close to 350 movies, and his acting abilities are different from Mohanlal. Although not as versatile, he brings a certain grace to his acting. While that might act as a restriction for him in terms of expanding his repertoire, he has done quite well in showcasing Malayalam cinema. In his late 60s, Mammootty shows no signs of slowing down and his actor son, Dulquer, has also carved out a niche for himself in Malayalam, Tamil and Telugu. Mammootty is not an active producer, but prefers collaborating with producers with whom he has a long-standing association. There is healthy competition and mutual respect between Mohanlal and Mammootty. They tend to compete at a creative level, which benefits the Malayalam industry in terms of the quality of its output. Between Prem Nazir, Mohanlal and Mammootty, there is an output close to 1,400 Malayalam movies, encapsulating the history of Malayalam cinema over the past seven decades. Unlike the Tamil and Telugu industries, the Malayalam industry is small in financial terms but grand in its creative contribution and technical excellence. There is a popular saying in the South Indian movie industry that the Tamil and Telugu cinema caters to the heart, whereas Malayalam cinema caters to the head.

Due to the limited production budgets and the financial necessity of sharing space and resources with other industries, the producer in the Malayalam industry did not evolve into an influential studio owner or media mogul. The scale of production remained small, with entrepreneurial producers operating at a small scale and with limited vision. What it lacks in commercial and financial clout, Malayalam cinema more than makes up for by punching above its weight through creative output and technical excellence.

Kannada movie industry

Juxtaposed with the commercial might of the Tamil and Telugu industries and the creative clout of Malayalam industry, the Kannada movie industry is still finding its feet and trying to establish a clear identity for itself (Kidiyoor and Yatgiri 2017). Initially based out of Madras, due to its geographic proximity to the state of Maharashtra, Kannada cinema was influenced by Marathi cinema. It was not uncommon, in British India, to complete the principal photography of a Kannada movie in and around the state of Bombay and then move to Madras for post-production. Since the early 1970s the Kannada industry gradually commenced its shift from Madras to Bangalore and, by the early 1980s, the shift was complete and the Kannada movie industry was operating from Bangalore. The geographic location of Karnataka state makes it an interesting cultural case study. Bordering Andhra Pradesh, Tamil Nadu and Maharashtra—three states that had strong language-based agitations to carve out separate identities— Karnataka did not get enough opportunities to establish its unique identity. Even in the present day, for Telugu and Tamil movies, the Karnataka market is significant and lucrative, but unfortunately not reciprocated, and Kannada movies are rarely seen on the screens of Tamil Nadu and Andhra Pradesh. Despite these constricting conditions, one individual worked relentlessly to put Kannada cinema on the map of Indian cinema.

Raj Kumar is not merely an individual in Kannada cinema, but an institution (Singh 2006). Having acted in close to 250 movies, Raj Kumar was also a prolific playback singer and since the early 1970s he has been singing in movies and has recorded more than 300 songs. Raj Kumar's wife Parvathama was a leading producer, producing several movies starring Raj Kumar and their three sons. The eldest son, Shiva, attained superstar status, closely followed by his youngest brother, Puneeth: also a major star in the Kannada industry. Raj Kumar's second son, Raghavendra, also acted in movies but has since retired. Beginning his early career in Madras, Raj Kumar was heavily influenced by AVM studios, Vijaya Vauhini and Gemini Studios and he closely observed the working style of these studio owners. This knowledge was put to good use when Raj Kumar launched his own production house in Bangalore. Raj Kumar is considered an icon of Kannada movies due to his significant contribution to the industry and endearingly affable and simple nature. He was the pioneer who championed the cause of a separate Kannada movie industry in Bangalore by shifting to Bangalore from Madras in the early 1970s and mentoring several newcomers to unearth talent in the industry. Apart from his acting and playback skills, Raj Kumar is fondly remembered for creating a Kannada movie ecosystem in Bangalore.

The Kannada movie ecosystem has successfully struck a balance between the commercial expectations of the box office and the artistic, creative expression sought after by connoisseurs of cinema. If Raj Kumar and his family present the commercial side of the Kannada cinema coin, B V Karanth, U R Ananthamurthy, Girish Kasaravalli, Anant Nag, Sankar Nag and Girish Karnad present the artistic side of it. The new wave cinema of India has a strong voice in Kannada cinema, and Girish Kasaravalli's *Ghatashraddha* (*The Ritual*) (Gopalan 2009) is a great example of using cinema as a mirror to focus on misguided social practices and customs. It is no coincidence that all the leading names of Kannada new wave cinema had their origins in theatre, and it was through treading the boards that they honed their storytelling abilities and brought them to the screen in the movies they conceived and created. However, the harsh realities and demands of the box office meant that such examples were few and far between, thereby forcing the proponents to explore avenues outside the landscapt of Kannada cinema. Karnataka is one state where the theatre culture is vibrant even today, and though this popularity is confined to the regions closer to Maharashtra, Kannada audiences are accustomed to reality in theatre and escapism in cinema. By nature, and historically, the Kannada audience is multilingual and this formed another stumbling block to Kannada cinema establishing strong roots.

Finally, significant responsibility for the commercial shortcomings of Kannada cinema lies in the hands of the Kannada moviemakers who dished out poor, cloned or recycled content, thereby making Kannada audiences yearn for originality. There was a phase in Kannada cinema when content predominantly focused on the underworld, mafia, murder and retribution stories, or shock-and-thrill mature content. This was off-putting for audiences who naturally migrated towards the Tamil, Telugu and Hindi movies that offered better options. With Bangalore becoming the software capital of India, it has acquired a pan-Indian, cosmopolitan image where Malayalam, Telugu, Hindi and Tamil are spoken on a par with Kannada, thereby creating demand for content from those languages. As the box office success of *Mungaru Male* (*Pre-monsoon Rain*) and *Ondu Motteye Katha* (*Story of an Egg Head*) proves, Kannada audiences are ready to accept content that is entertaining and thought-provoking. The time is ripe for Kannada cinema to come out of the claustrophobic commercial shadows of its neighbours so that it can carve out a niche and a distinct identity for itself without compromising the artistic freedom that cinema bestows on its advocates.

Conclusion

By taking a closer look at the Hindi, Bengali, Tamil, Telugu, Malayalam and Kannada industries, we presented the rich tapestry of movies and languages that are part of the Indian movie industry landscape. Viewed through the prism of regionalism, it is astonishing to think how entrepreneurial producers have pulled the industry together and made it not only national but global. Though the Punjabi, Marathi, Bhojpuri, Oriya and other smaller industries were not covered, it is important to note that they play a significant role in the growth and evolution of the Indian movie industry. In his reminiscence, the late entrepreneur Mr B Nagi Reddy (2013), founder of Vijaya Vauhini Studios, said that many shades make a rainbow and the Indian movie industry is a rainbow that has Hindi, Bengali, Tamil, Telugu, Malayalam, Kannada and other language movies as its many shades. Though this chapter began with a history of the different 'woods' of the Indian movie industry, it concludes with the statement that the Indian movie industry is much more vibrant and diverse than Hollywood. Calling the different industries operating under the Indian movie industry 'woods' is a disservice to the entrepreneurs as well as artists, technicians and the movie-loving public who built the Indian movie industry. The US$24 (EY 2019) billion media and entertainment industry in India deserves better than being dumbed down to just another 'wood'.

References

Ajithkumar, PK 2010, 'Evergreen Hero', *The Hindu*, 5 December, accessed 30/05/19, www.thehindu.com/todays-paper/tp-features/tp-fridayreview/The-evergreen-hero/art icle15936813.ece.
ANR n.d., quoted on www.annapurnastudios.com.
Ashokamithran 2002, *My Years with the Boss*, Orient Longman, Chennai, India.
Baskaran, ST 1981, *The Message Bearers: The Nationalist Politics and the Entertainment Media in South India*, Cre-A, Madras, India.
Baskaran, ST 2009, *History through the Lens: Perspectives on South Indian Cinema*, Orient Blackswan, Chennai, India.

Bhatia, S 2012, 'Rajesh Khanna: Bollywood's first superstar', *BBC News*, 18 July, accessed 27/10/18, www.bbc.com/news/world-asia-india-18738482.

Cain, R 2015, 'India's movie industry—A $10 billion business trapped in a $2 billion body', *Forbes*, 23 October, accessed 26/10/18, https://www.forbes.com/sites/robcain/2015/10/23/indias-film-industry-a-10-billion-business-trapped-in-a-2-billion-body/#73018ecb70d2.

Central Board of Movie Certification 2017, *Annual Report April 2016 to March 2017*. Ministry of Information and Broadcasting, Government of India, accessed 27/10/18, www.cbfcindia.gov.in/main/CBFC_English/Attachments/AR_2016-17_English.pdf.

Chabria, S, Usai, PC and Virchand, D 1994, *Light of Asia: Indian Silent Cinema, 1912–1934*, NFAI.Pune, India.

Chandran, KN 1994, 'Literacy in India and the example of Kerala', *Journal of Reading*, vol. 37, no. 6, pp. 514–517.

Chowdhury, AR 2018, 'Revisiting Naxalbari: Narratives of violence and exclusions from the marginal spaces', in A Bhattacharyya and S Basu (eds), *Marginalities in India*, pp. 81–94, Springer, Singapore.

Dalrymple, W 2019, *The Anarchy: The Relentless Rise of the East India Company*, Bloomsbury, London.

Dasu, KR, 2004, 'The Mother of all rath yatras', *The Hindu*, 1 April, accessed 26/10/18, www.thehindu.com/2004/04/01/stories/2004040100991200.htm.

Dickey, S 1993, 'The politics of adulation: Cinema and the production of politicians in South India', *The Journal of Asian Studies*, vol. 52, no. 2, pp. 340–372.

Dickey, S 1995, 'Consuming utopia: Movie-Watching in Tamil Nadu', in C Breckenridge (ed), *Consuming Modernity*, pp. 131–156, University of Minnesota Press, Minneapolis, MN.

EY 2019, 'A billion screens of opportunity', Report published for Federation of Indian Chamber of Commerce and Industry (FICCI), Mumbai, India.

Ganti, T 2013, *Bollywood: A Guidebook to Popular Hindi Cinema*, 2nd Edn, Routledge, New York.

Gopalakrishnan, A 1985, *The Rat Trap—Elipathayam*, Translated by S.Banerjee, Seagull books, Calcutta, India.

Gopalan, L 2009, *The Cinema of India*, Wallflower Press, New York.

Guy, R 2016, *Memories of Madras: Its Movies, Musicians and Men of Letters*, pp. 3–41, Creative Workshop, Chennai, India.

Jaffe, G and Doshi, V, 2017, 'One of the few places where a communist can still dream', *Washington Post*, 27 October, accessed 27/10/18, https://www.washingtonpost.com/world/asia_pacific/the-place-where-communists-can-still-dream/2017/10/26/55747cbe-9c98-11e7-b2a7-bc70b6f98089_story.html.

Kidiyoor, GH and Yatgiri, PV 2017, '*Kannada Movie Industry in India: Strategies for Survival*', *Emerald Emerging Markets Case Studies*, vol. 7, no. 3, pp. 1–27..

Krishen, P 1991, 'Knocking at the doors of public culture: India's parallel cinema', *Public Culture*, vol. 4, no. 1, pp. 25–41.

Meiyappan, AV 2015, *My Experiences in Life*, AVM Charities, Chennai, India.

Murthy, CHSN 2017, 'Telugu diaspora as soft power: Mapping media, cultural ties and political economy with homeland', *Diaspora Studies*, vol. 10, pp. 97–115.

Nathan, A 2018, 'At Ramoji Movie City in Hyderabad, everything is about show business (and not just for moviemakers)', *Scroll in*, 6 February, accessed 26/10/18, https://scroll.in/reel/860202/location-scouting-everything-is-about-show-business-at-ramoji-movie-city-not-just-for-moviemakers.

Nayar, BR 2006, 'When did the Hindu rate of growth end?', *Economic and Political Weekly*, vol. 14, no. 19, pp. 1885–1890.

Prasad, M 2003, 'This thing called Bollywood', *Seminar* 525, accessed 24/05/19, www.india-seminar.com.

Rao, PG 2000, 'Tax reform in India: Achievements and challenges', *Asia Pacific Development Journal*, vol. 7, no. 2, pp. 59–74.

Reddi, BN 2013, *Many Shades Make a Rainbow*, Vijaya Publications, Chennai, India.

Saraswathi, S 2013, 'Looking at the dying studios of Chennai', *Rediff Movies*, 18 September, accessed 26/10/18, www.rediff.com/movies/report/slide-show-1-looking-at-the-dying-studios-of-chennai/20130918.htm.

Singh, K 2006, 'Rajkumar: Demigod of Southern Indian Movie', accessed 27/10/18, www.independent.co.uk/news/obituaries/rajkumar-6103761.html.

PART II

India's entrepreneurial movie business

Producers and their circle

3
ENTREPRENEURIAL MOVIE PRODUCERS IN INDIA

Cinema in India is like brushing your teeth; you can't escape it.
Shahrukh Khan, India's leading actor

Making a movie is a terribly painful experience.
George Lucas, creator of Star Wars

Introduction

In emerging economies such as India, growth in entrepreneurship is occurring. This is due to the economic conditions in the country and new technologies creating fresh opportunities, in some instances due to government support and, in many cases, despite lack of government support. As detailed in Chapter 2, Indian movie production is concentrated in clusters located in big cities. Not all the entrepreneurial Indian producers in this book originated from big cities like Mumbai, Chennai, Kolkata, Bengaluru and Hyderabad but they have set up their production houses in these cities because of the necessity to operate within an existing cluster or ecosystem. Producers from the Malayalam movie industry operating from a second-tier city, Kochi, are also part of the book but those from smaller cities like Amritsar for Punjabi and Cuttack for Oriya are omitted for reasons of access, space and scope.

The failure rate in the movie industry is high and can be compared with the venture-capitalist adage that nine in ten new ventures will fail. However, due to the multiple revenue streams available to movie producers today, if the production budget is under control, the chances of success increase. It might not be accurate to say that Indian movie producers are prepared for failure, but they are certainly more accustomed to failure. A cursory glance at the Internet Movie

Database (imdb.com), recognised as an industry standard, reveals that there are more flops and disasters than hits and blockbusters. So Indian movie producers are well-aware of the failure rate but still choose to make the industry their entrepreneurial pathway.

Behind the glitz and glamour, there is a significant amount of sweat and effort that goes into getting a movie project off the ground and into theatres. Before mapping out the producer's entrepreneurial journey, it is essential to appreciate the ecosystem of the movie industry and its key players. Renowned British ecologist Sir Arthur Tansley (1871–1955), Professor of Botany at Oxford, a pioneer in the science of ecology, coined the word 'ecosystem' in the year 1935. Ecosystem as a concept was devised to shine a spotlight on how organisms survive, thrive and wither away in an environment by transferring materials. The intention was to focus not only on the organism and the environment but also on the various factors that comprise an environment. An ecosystem in the context of this book considers the external factors that aid the entrepreneur's success or failure, acting as enablers or inhibitors to the creation of new services or goods. Entrepreneurs mostly undertake their business in localities in which they live and work, only later moving to more distant locations, suggesting that the ecosystem is influential for start-ups prepared to take risks (Audretsch et al. 2018; O' Connor et al. 2018) such as producing new movies. Entrepreneurial ecosystems provide a framework for understanding the nature of locations in which entrepreneurial activity flourishes, like the regions which support Indian movies.

Examining the popular tool of the entrepreneurial ecosystem helps understand the reason why a particular geographic region experiences high entrepreneurial activity. Ecosystems are a harmonious amalgamation and combination of local culture, availability of capital, social network, academic institutions and policymakers' decisions that support the creation of ventures within a domain (Isenberg 2010). The most commonly cited attributes of entrepreneurial ecosystems can be grouped into cultural, social and material categories, depending on the manner in which benefits are accrued and administered (Spigel 2017). For the past 123 years, ever since the Lumiere brothers made the first movie in 1896, the movie industry has typically operated in geographical ecosystems. Though there might be several reasons behind forming these ecosystems, the most important reasons are the availability of land, easy access, infrastructure and pooling of talent. The previous chapter presented in detail the different industries that combine to form the Indian movie industry; this chapter embeds the ecosystem within the framework of the various players who contribute to the success (or failure) of the entrepreneurial producer's movie ventures. We integrate the theoretical lens with the key players in the ecosystem who create social and economic value and provide conditions for success (Sarma and Sunny 2017).

The producers

A movie is touted to be the director's vision in partnership with an entrepreneurial opportunity-seeker known as the producer. The director is labelled as captain of the cinema ship while the producer champions a new idea, creates new product and takes it to the market. Together, the director and producer are a creative and entrepreneurial team. Stars receive all the screen space, adulation and lifestyle-altering effects, come success or failure. Technicians are well-paid and become professionals in their craft, honing their skills with each movie. There seems to be a missing link here: is the director the connection between all the moving parts of movie production? No, the director's job is to direct the movie. Then is the star responsible for all the organised chaos of movie production? No, a star is a vehicle that has to carry the movie and ensure a good opening weekend. So, who is responsible for each and every aspect of a movie, right from when the idea is conceived to when it is declared a hit or a flop? The answer to this question is: the producer. The producer is the link between all the moving parts of movie production; the producer is the one responsible for ensuring that the organised chaos does not disintegrate into a disorganised disaster. If the producer is not entrepreneurial, balancing the needs of recognising and implementing a good idea, bringing together the pieces of the puzzle, as well as the much-needed money, then a high-risk venture may not get off the ground.

According to the Global Entrepreneurship Monitor, entrepreneurs' motivations can be divided into opportunity and necessity (Mota, Braga, and Ratten 2019). Opportunity and necessity (Van der Zwan et al. 2016) can be motivating factors for entrepreneurs to enter into movie production. It is essential to understand the role played by motivation in creating new production houses or organisations in the movie industry. All the second-generation producers had the necessity of running an existing business and turning it around from the verge of bankruptcy, or using the platform as an opportunity to expand and grow the business. There are movie producers who get into the business as a choice, i.e., opportunity. They may choose to enter the movie industry due to necessity or an interest that encourages them to shift from a different industry to the movie industry. Entrepreneurial movie producers in India are a colourful bunch and can be categorised into three types. Table 3.1 illustrates the three types of entrepreneurs—Start-up, Lifestyle and Family Business—providing a summary of background and focus of enterprise. The first type is the Start-up entrepreneur movie producer. This type of producer selects movie production as their entrepreneurial vehicle. They tend to be younger, willing to take bigger risks and also change some of the operational customs in the industry. They are willing to be professional and come with experience in a different industry (e.g., engineering, business finance). The second type is the Lifestyle entrepreneur movie producer. This type of producer has an alternative career, is generally successful and lucrative, and enters movie production for the sake of creative

TABLE 3.1 Types of entrepreneurs in the Indian movie industry

Type	Background	Enterprise
Start-up	The producers of this type of Indian movie business are alert, agile, energetic, innovative, and financially and artistically willing to take risks. They bring in a culture of professionalism and breaking away from established conventions in terms of both content and execution.	The enterprise is characterised by being small, nimble, flexible, digitally enabled and adept, employing young and digitally savvy directors and scriptwriters, with a continuing core of employees as well as flexible project workers employed movie to movie. It has a global reach.
Lifestyle	Mid-career producer with a professional background in education (e.g., MBA, Chartered Accountant, Architect) who operates the business on his/her terms and indulges in movie production as a lifestyle choice and as a second business, rather than the main vocation.	Make movies with specific taste and preferences, willing to take calculated risks but sticking to their convictions and beliefs. Indulging in the business for passion or for the glamour and visibility. Tends to loan team members from the parent organisation and other vocations, thereby bringing an unbiased approach.
Family Business	Early to mid-career movie producer with a background in engineering, film school, photography, etc., continuing the family business. Makes movies in numerous Indian languages for regional screening. Passionate and persistent despite a mix of successes and failures over the years and zealously guarding the legacy built by father/grandfather.	Family business established by founder producer, financed by the family firm and belonging to the second or third generation, which aspires to make more than five movies per year. Seeks to grow with investor funds but tends to be risk-averse and always toying with the idea of professionalising the enterprise so that family owns it but professionals manage.

interest in the art and passion for the medium; sheer opportunism; or to bask in the limelight. Their background is more likely to be in the creative industries, such as architecture, film school or photography. Such entrepreneurs can even be changing careers after a self-assessment (Obodaru 2012) that resulted in a realisation they are not happy with their current career status and want to venture into something different. The third type is the Family Business entrepreneur movie producer. This type of producer is continuing the legacy established by father or grandfather (no women in this case) and normally tends to build on the success, credibility, connections and infrastructure built by earlier generations. Their background is more likely to be in movies, due to the long family tradition of success in the Indian movie business.

A brief snapshot of movie producers and their circle interviewed for this book is provided in Tables 3.2 and 3.3. Producers range from very experienced and senior producers who commenced operations during the black-and-white print

TABLE 3.2 Snapshot of Indian movie producers interviewed

Role	Gender	Experience	Movies and years of experience
Producers (first and second generation)	Male (26)	Postgraduates, undergraduates and high school graduates with expertise in a range of backgrounds from movies to accountancy, business, engineering, architecture, computer science and photography. All have Indian nationality but three have significant experience in the USA that informed their Indian producers' role.	Between three and 170 movies over a period of six decades.
Producer (first generation; married to an actor)	Female (1)	Postgraduate with expertise as a child counsellor and producer. Indian nationality.	Six movies over 23 years.

TABLE 3.3 Snapshot of producers' circle interviewed

Role	Gender	Experience	Movies and years of experience
Producers' circle from first generation to third generation)	Male (12)	Postgraduates and high school graduates who have expertise as film critics and reviewers, movie editors, distributors, exhibitors, TV-channel executives, movie publicity executives and movie directors. All are of Indian nationality, but one has significant experience in the USA that informed his Indian experience.	Between five and 172 movies over 50 years.
Producers' circle (one first generation; one second generation)	Female (2)	Postgraduates with expertise as film critics, film reviewers and sub-titling specialists. Both are Indian nationality.	Up to 500 movies in more than 20 years' working experience.

era, to those who have moved on to colour, CinemaScope, 70 mm prints and finally digital. Of the 27 producers interviewed, 26 were male, and only one was female. They ranged in age from the early thirties to early eighties and had produced between three and 170 movies. Those interviewed produced movies in all four South Indian languages, demonstrating the reach and spread of the Indian movie industry. In other words, producers interviewed were from

Bollywood, Kollywood, Tollywood (the one located in Hyderabad), Mollywood and Sandalwood. The average age of the producers interviewed was mid-fifties. Most producers had a tertiary qualification. However, six had become producers after completing high school. Of the people interviewed in the producers' circle, most had a tertiary qualification, with three having only a high school qualification. In this latter group, again, men dominated: we interviewed ten men and three women.

As the table illustrates, movie producers vary in age and expertise, background, number of movies produced and years in the business. It can be seen from this that they have varying experience of an entrepreneurial nature. However, there is one overwhelming fact: most independent movie producers are male, as stated previously.

Those in the producers' circle include one more woman (a ratio of 2:13), again with most having tertiary education (11:3). They come from a range of backgrounds, such as movie critic, movie editor, movie sub-titling specialist, distributor, TV-channel executive, movie publicity expert, exhibitor and movie director. In these roles, they have worked on between five and 500 movies.

All Indian movie industry professionals mentioned are independent, though some of them worked in multinational corporations and large corporate houses. None of them are new to the industry, with experience ranging from five years to 65 years. Put together, this book captures the experience of more than 1,000 movies.

Themes emerging from the interviews

We cover the five key themes from our interviews in this section.

Theme 1: producers and the entrepreneurial process

A movie producer must exhibit command over creativity in script selection, budgeting, project management and marketing in order to execute a movie project successfully. These four roles fit in well with Shane's (2003) theory of entrepreneurship that highlights the discovery of opportunity, execution and exploitation. Building on the ideas initially presented by Venkataraman (1997), Shane defines entrepreneurship as 'an activity that involves the discovery, evaluation and exploitation of opportunities to introduce new goods and services, ways of organizing, markets, processes, and raw materials through organizing efforts that previously had not existed' (p. 4). The nub of the theory examines the nexus between opportunity and entrepreneurial individuals who identify opportunities in the process. Entrepreneurship is more than a function of different types of people engaging in entrepreneurial activity but also entails identifying opportunities and capitalising on them (Shane 2003). In the movie industry, opportunity recognition is evident in identifying a script that has the potential to be a blockbuster. One mid-career movie producer who, interestingly, was an engineer, shared the following insight about the importance of script selection: 'I never went into production without completely finalising the script, though this delayed my output, it ensured that I had a quality product.'

Execution is the process of producing a movie, and exploitation is the process of marketing and revenue generation to recover the costs incurred. Therefore, for every movie produced, a movie producer is an entrepreneur in the true sense.

This was pointed out by a young movie producer who has questioned the status quo and created a systematic professional approach to moviemaking. This producer was an architect and made a career change when he became fascinated with the 'architecture of moviemaking'. As he explained in this quote, he discusses the four verticals of moviemaking by which he means the four functions of a movie producer:

> Very early on, we said that there will be four verticals within the office. Though I might be doing probably three of them, I still know that these are clear verticals. Content creation is a clear vertical, I know when there is a full-bound script, that's when this vertical gets completed. Then there is content execution, which is like production, which is very industrious, process-oriented; we make all these things. Then again, we go back into a creative zone which is the marketing, the designing and, you know, advertising and things like that. That is a clear vertical; saying that even at the beginning of the thing, we used to design the logo, font, poster, what we are going to sell this movie with. So, we had a very strong idea in terms of marketing, then obviously the final vertical is the sale, how do you sell and generate maximum revenue.

By verticals, he refers to the four functions of a movie producer, and he discusses them as 'content creation', 'content execution', 'content marketing' and, finally, 'business development and selling', effectively summing up the entrepreneurial process of movie production.

Theme 2: movie production culture

Entrepreneurship in moviemaking can be embedded in the broader domain of cultural entrepreneurship. The basic tenets of entrepreneurship as listed by Timmons et al. (1987)—opportunity recognition, resource allocation and team formation—remain constant in cultural entrepreneurship through moviemaking. Entrepreneurship is centred on opportunities; every other factor, like money, team and strategy is secondary compared to an opportunity. We refer to the definition of cultural entrepreneurship as proposed by Lounsbury and Glynn (2001) who asserted that at the core of every entrepreneurial activity is a process of meaning-making, like narrating stories through movies that tend to construct a distinct identity. Opportunity is more important than the lead entrepreneur or the team. In the case of the movie industry, the script and the casting are that opportunity. If the script is excellent and the right cast is found for that script, then the producer's job becomes easier. If the right script is in hand, it is like identifying a good opportunity; then the resources can be managed even with the bare minimum available. A movie producer, after identifying the opportunity, should be able to raise the necessary funds and put together a good team to execute the project. From personal experience, having a good script in hand, or having the dates of a leading star ensures that the project will move forward. The winning combination is a good script and a leading actor. In the context of Indian cinema, until the late 1990s, scripts were viewed as secondary compared to star power. This resulted in poor quality movies that were riding on the star's image rather than on a good script. However, in the last two decades there has been a perceptible change in this trend, particularly when leading actors started giving the script the prominent place it deserves and only accepting ventures with good scripts. When opportunity knocks in the form of a good script, the Indian movie producer today can rest assured that the resources and right cast or set of actors will find their way to that script.

In the case of cultural entrepreneurship, especially in the Indian movie industry, it is interesting to note the significant impact and role played by actors who can access and employ different elements of culture in an ingenious way to control and influence the behaviour and thought processes of their followers or fans who are taken in by the 'cultural turn' (Friedland and Mohr 2004). The cultural turn refers to the manner in which the audience tends to believe the on-screen persona of the actor and start worshipping that persona. This, in a way, explains why many leading actors have success as politicians and elected representatives. As explained by a producer,

> They don't even understand, they are not able to distinguish the industry from the creative element of the industry so that mix up is there. You like a star because you like a character he played in some film. You are not able to distinguish between the role and the actual person, so it is a difference between the creator/director and the creation that gets confused. That is there with everybody, no exception.

This producer was a financier and a mid-career producer who had produced 20 movies in the past ten years, with high-status qualifications in engineering and business. He appreciated that the dream he was peddling was an important factor in his success.

Movie entrepreneurs perfectly fit into the category of both sense-makers and sense-givers (Gioia and Chittipeddi 1991). They are sense-makers because their stories and scripts tend to be influenced by society, and they create sense for themselves by the changes taking place in society. They are sense-givers because their movies, in turn, tend to influence society and present a cinematic version of the society that made sense to the producer and they want to share and give that sense to society in general. Cinema is undoubtedly a part of culture or symbolic of its culture; it is no exaggeration to state that many viewers across the world are influenced, rightly or wrongly, by Hollywood movies when it comes to how they perceive US society (Moody 2017). A second-generation producer summed it up by stating that, '[The] movie is the cheapest form of entertainment in India and for less than US$2 an Indian movie can provide entertainment as well as cultural sense.'

Taking a more pragmatic view, it can be argued that movie producers have chosen cinema as a medium for their entrepreneurial journey and are making use of the cultural resources offered by movies in order to build an organisation. Both senior and junior producers agree that the 'movie is the most attractive option to get into the limelight and build an organisation'. The Walt Disney Corporation, in its relentless pursuit to be the behemoth of entertainment, is a classic example of using movies as a medium to build a business conglomerate, with the acquisition of Pixar and Marvel serving as goalposts in this pursuit. The contours of cultural entrepreneurship have been broadened and the focus expanded from the Bill Gates and Steve Jobs type of path-breaking technology entrepreneurs to more routine and everyday types of entrepreneurs (Aldrich and Ruef 2017); movie producers were and are still part of this category. Cultural entrepreneurship in movies in countries like India does indeed address the bottom-of-the-pyramid problems. It might be just an interesting coincidence that the person who coined the phrase 'fortune at the bottom of the pyramid', Coimbatore Krishnarao Prahlad, or the late CK Prahlad, originates from Tamil Nadu, one of the most prolific movie-producing regions in the world. Cultural entrepreneurship in movies in India tends to have outcomes related to social and cultural innovation (Lounsbury and Glynn 2019). Dress and fashion, technology, utopian conceptes and advances, and the mobilising of the masses were all strongly influenced by the movie industry in India. It is common for girls to imitate leading ladies and boys to imitate the leading men in terms of personality and personal appearance. A senior movie producer pointed this out: 'By just having stills of heroines on my movie posters, fashion trends used to be started.'

Therefore, movie entrepreneurship aids and abets value creation that forms benchmarks for future generations to refine, reconstruct and build on identity. Value creation can be two dimensional: first, creating social values that are ideal for society and for the betterment of members in that society; second, the economic dollar-value of the industry that makes it an attractive career option for future generations of aspiring entrepreneurs. Three producers we interviewed were elected to the position of President of the South Indian Film Chamber of Commerce, one of those three producers who started as a production assistant pointed out, 'The movies I produced gave me an identity and that identity helped me occupy such an important post through which I could serve the society.'

From humble beginnings, this producer grew in stature to eventually have a very good personal rapport with the Chief Minister of the State, which in turn benefitted the movie community and society in general. The benefits to society included free medical insurance and health benefits for all family members of movie workers. Before the introduction of this insurance scheme, the families of movie workers who were injured or who lost their lives were left destitute. Thereby, the cultural impact of a *Sholay* or a *Baahubali* is far more significant than the box office numbers alone. So this is a unique feature of movie entrepreneurship in a developing nation like India and differentiates it from entrepreneurship in other domains in other developed countries.

Theme 3: producer and their team

The producer dons the hats of pragmatist, problem solver, human resource manager and profit seeker. The producer works with cast, crew and financiers as part of a team. They cannot do it alone. The producer is someone who is aware of reality; this reality can be expressed in terms of the financial aspects—like the amount of money available to spend—or the practical aspects, as in a certain shooting location being available. However, the director will have a vision for the movie and would like to convey it onto the screen as close as possible to their original vision. The producer plays a crucial role in aligning the director's vision with reality and yet ensuring that the finished product has the desired impact on its viewers. A young US-trained Indian producer who returned to India to make his movies nailed it when he said, 'If the director's vision is not aligned to the producer's goal, then there is a high chance of an impending disaster.'

Another distinguishing feature of a producer is their metaphorical fire-fighting ability to put out fires that are intentionally or unintentionally caused by the cast and crew. In these situations, the business acumen and experience of the producer kicks in and helps them to know what to do when things go awry. Moviemaking is a complex process that juxtaposes human creativity, ingenuity and human shortcomings, such as ego and megalomania. A senior producer lamented, 'I lost 20 years of my earnings and savings in one movie because of the megalomania of one leading actor and director; I had to start from scratch after 20 years because they did not see reason.'

Obviously, it was a very painful experience but not an uncommon one for movie producers. On sets during production, the producer is the central link that connects all the cast and crew members, thereby carrying the burden of managing all the relationships and ensuring there is transparent and continuous communication. Many producers allot a few days before the actual shooting commences to hold ice-breaking sessions or workshops for the cast and crew to develop a good working relationship and to ensure that everyone is working towards the same goal. Finally, a producer dons the hat of businessman to ensure that the movie maximises its revenue potential by collaborating with the right set of distributors and exhibitors who will showcase the product with the aim of attracting maximum eyeballs. A semi-retired second-generation producer summed it up by saying that,

> The revenue potential of a movie has to be harnessed to the maximum possible potential and I detest the manner in which some producers are giving up their rights perpetually whereas they could financially benefit by selling the rights for a limited period.

The producer plans for the short-term as well as the long-term revenue monetisation through theatrical rights, satellite rights, streaming and digital rights, merchandising, in-movie product placement, syndication and remake rights. All this is done by building a team of key players and supporters who together manage ego, megalomania and risk through their vision and by making the most of the entrepreneurial opportunities.

Theme 4: male bastion, wives and daughters

In the Hollywood context, it has been 100 years since United Artists was formed as a studio with the basic premise that artists should be allowed the freedom to control their own interests. There were four partners in this enterprise: Charles Chaplin, D W Griffith, Douglas Fairbanks and Mary Pickford. Yes, 100 years ago, there was a female entrepreneur in the movie industry. Pickford was a pioneer in many ways. As well as being a talented actor, a very popular box office drawcard and a founding member of the Academy of Motion Picture Arts and Sciences, Pickford was entrepreneurial in her outlook and believed in the potential of cinema as a medium of entertainment. A famous quote attributed to her sums up her philosophy: 'Failure is not the falling down but staying down'. Unfortunately, in the past 100 years, not many women have followed in the path of Pickford. Even though, over the past 20 years, the percentage of women producers has increased, female producers still make up fewer than 30 per cent of producers in Hollywood (Lauzen 2019). Despite more than 50 per cent of the US population being women, there is a significant gap between the genders in Hollywood film and television production (Erigha 2015). The inclusion of all technical roles still does not help their cause, as fewer than 18 per cent of such roles are performed by women (Lauzen 2019). Though several reasons might be attributed to the under-representation of women in the role of producer, it is a fact that women producers are few and far between.

This fact is evident in Indian cinema too, where female producers are far rarer than in Hollywood. The reasons for low representation can be cultural, social and economic. The reason for low representation, from a cultural perspective, is that Indian culture is rooted in the large bodies of spiritual texts called the Vedas, which propagated the myth that a woman is defined by her birth and her marriage; therefore her independence is not to be encouraged. This has always been a major obstacle for women movie producers. Secondly, from a social perspective, the movie industry was viewed as a lower-value profession and women from respectable families did not act or take part in it. Many decades ago, when the Indian caste system was rigid, upper-caste women were prohibited from even attending movie screenings. Therefore, for many years, male actors dressed up as females to portray female characters. With the increased popularity of theatre and cinema, lower-caste women ventured into acting because they found the remuneration to be lucrative. It took many decades for these shackles to be broken and there is a perceptible change now, but even when viewed in the broader context of the low number of women entrepreneurs, the number of women producers is low. And thirdly, from an economic perspective, in a male-dominated Indian society women did not have access to funds and resources, thereby curtailing their ability to launch ventures. This was further amplified in the movie industry where the failure rate was high, and women did not want to risk the meagre resources that they had access to.

Hence the industry was perceived as male-dominated and not an attractive career option, behind the camera, for women. Though the number of female directors has increased, the number of female producers has not undergone much significant change. A majority of the female movie producers in Indian cinema tend to be spouses or children of leading male actors who have taken up the mantle to assist their husbands or fathers. For example, one female producer explains how she became a producer:

> My husband is an actor, after certain years he wanted to produce a film. First, he directed a film and there was a producer from the US. So, he started the production, and everything was going on and suddenly he abandoned the project and left the country, so we had to take it over and my husband had to take up the responsibility of releasing this movie. He went from pillar to post and somehow arranged all the funds for releasing the movie and by default I ended up as the movie producer.

In Chapter 2, Raj Kumar and his family were profiled while detailing the Kannada film industry. All the movies produced by Raj Kumar and his sons had Mrs Parvathamma Raj Kumar listed as the producer. She has produced 80 movies and was the leading female producer in India until her passing in 2017. Ekta Kapoor, daughter of yesteryear star Jeetendra is currently the leading female producer in India. She has produced more than 40 movies and more than 100 television shows. In the Telugu movie industry, Vijaya Nirmala holds the Guinness World Record for the most number of movies directed by a female (42), and she also produced, along with her husband, Krishna, under the banner of Sri Vijaya Krishna movies. Bhanumathi and Savithri, both leading actresses, produced movies in South India during the 1950s, 1960s and 1970s.

Current female movie producers represent their husband's interests. This again reiterates the earlier statement that the majority of female producers in India tend to be actresses who produce their own movies or continue producing after they stop acting, or are daughters of producers, directors and actors or wives of producers, directors and actors. The notable exception to this trend is Guneet Monga, a first-generation professional movie producer who has carved out a niche for herself by independently producing creative content that achieves commercial success as well as critical acclaim. Her last production won the Academy Award for Best Documentary. Guneet stands out as a rare exception that has made a mark as a producer by sheer commitment and effort.

The sole female producer's experience presents a different perspective:

> The sad part was that I was pregnant at that time, I was going around asking for business settlement and this gentleman never gave any settlement and he said he owes seven million rupees to all the distributors, so I literally fought with everybody and I went to the producers' council and that was when I joined the producers' council. I know that we can sort out our problems only through the producers' council. Of course, they helped me out a lot at that time. Because one woman coming every day to sort out the problem, they felt bad for me, first time producer. So, I sorted out, because I wanted to do the next film, unless this is sorted out because I want to be with clean hands to do the next film. I don't want to carry over to another film, finally I cleared up everything.

This quote exemplifies the way in which female producers have to go the extra mile just to be heard. This female producer had to enrol in the peak trade body to have a voice and to feel empowered. In other words, she needed men of influence in powerful positions behind her in order to receive the money which was owed to her. There is a long way to go for female producers in India.

While only one female producer was interviewed, a senior second-generation producer's son, and now his grand-daughters, are taking up the mantle of production and continuing the legacy of their well-known brand. These young women have had their entrepreneurial journey anchored in a family business, reducing the risk for them as female producers, protecting them from the travails of a start-up and the difficulties of being a woman in a male-dominated industry. The grandfather summed it up as such: 'A new generation has to take up the mantle and then only new ideas and new methods will come in and will ensure the survival of this industry.'

Although researching the reasons for low participation of women in the movie industry across the world is beyond the scope of this book, we hope that, with the number of female students in movie and media schools increasing significantly, it is only a matter of time before the number of women venturing into movie production will also increase.

Theme 5: passion for cinema

Why does a producer produce a movie? This is a question that has been put to several producers over the decades because when a movie ends being a disaster, critics and audience wonder what is driving this need to produce a movie. Passion is a word that is heard often in the movie industry; it is a common theme that keeps recurring in all the conversations with Indian movie producers. A majority of movie producers cited passion as the main factor that pushed them to battle the odds and keep going despite failures. From a distance, a movie producer's passion might seem harmonious (Vallerand 2015) but in reality there is a strong hint of obsession (Fisher, Merlot and Johnson 2018). One of the producers was clear and forthright in emphasising that he was so obsessed with wiping out the memories of a colossal box office failure he had suffered that he pushed himself to produce four more movies in order to recoup every rupee lost in the flop. In fact, he did not rest until he achieved that goal, exhibiting obsessive traits. At the other end of the spectrum there is another producer who was forced to make peace with his debilitating failures and show harmonious passion (Vallerand et al. 2003) when he was forced to make peace with his past failures and move out of movie production rather than face failure again in a new venture.

One second-generation movie producer who represented India in several international film festivals described the passion for cinema in a nutshell:

> If we have passion for film making nothing will stop, you and we will keep on making films. End of the day, we had human beings who worked with us, people wanted their films to run not to just make money.

This can be passion for using the visual medium to convey a message; passion for moulding a written script into moving images; or passion for suspending disbelief. A mid-career movie producer who worked as a senior executive in other industries before taking up movie production put it like this:

> Movies was the only world that existed for me from the age of four when I used to accompany my mother to the movies. As I grew up my love for movies became a passion and anyone who knew me was not surprised as I became a producer because it was natural progression for me.

A producer produces movies with a passion for the 'art of cinema'; a producer produces movies with the passion of a businessman to make money in the commercial sense, and a producer produces movies with the passion for gaining fame and access to celebrities. As a senior producer who has produced more than 25 movies commented:

> If you are in the movie industry just for money then the industry will not take care of you, but if you are in it for the passion of moviemaking then you will somehow survive and be looked after.

Curiously, this producer did not attain fame or fortune but still persisted in the industry due to his love and passion for the craft. He began his entrepreneurial journey 36 years ago with start-up capital of one million rupees in cash (worn on a waist belt) provided by his father. He lost the capital in its entirety in his first production. He had no training and did not plan and execute the production. Since then, he has learnt by trial and error and has had varying degrees of success.

All these are valid reasons for an individual to become a movie producer. If the reason and the goal are clear, then the chances of failure may be reduced. As George Lucas commented, movie production is a painful experience. It is an apt expression summarising the entire process. Some producers experience less pain because of planning and execution, while others experience great pain due to the best-laid plans going awry. In conclusion, it is important to state that a movie cannot be made without a producer. For more than 100 years, the role of a producer has been constantly changing and evolving.

Hollywood has popularised the model of studios running productions. In such cases, the studio is the main financier and the studio appoints a producer who performs several functions but assumes limited financial risk. Whereas, in the Indian movie industry, a majority of producers are independent producers and they assume almost the complete financial risk.

The concluding section of this chapter briefly discusses the roles of line producer and executive producer.

Line producer

In the Indian movie industry, a movie production relies significantly on the expertise and managerial abilities of a production manager. It is no exaggeration to state that the production manager is the person who will ensure that the project is either completed within budget or ends up coming in over budget. Though the nomenclature of production manager and line producer are used interchangeably, the job description is similar and line producer is a universally accepted job title. Once the script is locked in and the movie is ready to go to the pre-production stage, the line producer will be one of the first crew members to be brought on board by the overall producer. The line producer is a vital cog in the wheel of movie production. Financial planning and operations-management roles are seamlessly integrated into one: the line producer. Once the budget is finalised, the line producer takes on the responsibility of managing the budget. Many established producers finalise the budget only after thorough discussion with and inputs from the line producer. A line producer can either hire a production manager to run the day-to-day production or, in many cases, the line producer doubles up on the production management role for better control and coordination. Unless there is a long-term relationship and rapport between the producer and the line producer, the line producer is not invited into creative discussions or to be part of the creative crew. Good line producers do not work on more than one project at a time, so that they can give their undivided attention to the project at hand. However, there are some line producers who juggle their time between two or more projects at a time, thereby negatively impacting the quality of their work.

The producer has the right to demand exclusive commitment from the line producer during the course of the production. A line producer generally hires key members of the crew, negotiates deals with vendors and is almost a de facto head of production, serving as the eyes and ears of the producer. Producers, typically, once brought in their family members, such as a brother or a close cousin, and entrusted them with production responsibility. This is largely due to trust deficit. Rather than trusting a professional member, producers are more comfortable trusting their own family because of the high stakes involved. Line producers are seldom involved in the script and creative development of the project, but always play a significant role in breaking up the cost structure and working out daily expenses for the production in order to reassure the cast and crew, and even the financiers, that the production is on track. As soon as the script is finalised and the finance is in place, the line producer works on preparing the movie's budget and daily scheduling. Professional line producers are usually employed on a project-to-project basis and although the role is respected and well remunerated, and includes the opportunity to set up an ancillary business, long hours and tough working conditions are the norm. Several line producers advance to the stage of independent producer, and, if they are a family member, a line producer is credited as a co-producer.

The title 'line producer' was coined because a person in this role was expected to know the difference between the costs that are incurred by the producer both above the line and below the line. Since they would be managing all production-related activities of a movie, they were expected to know, in-depth, all the relevant costs from the above-the-line costs, like remuneration to director, technicians and cast, to the below-the-line costs, which in a sense include everything else (i.e., the cost of set design and erection, support-crew wages, cine equipment rental and other development costs). Generally, the producer handles the above-the-line costs and finalises the remuneration packages for the leading cast, director and important technicians. A line producer will not be involved in these negotiations unless they are a family member. However, once above-the-line costs are finalised, the line producer will be given access to the script and tasked with the responsibility of assessing the below-the-line cost of production. This will lead to the next step of fixing schedules and shooting dates according to the screenplay and shot delineation. From these schedules, the line producer can accurately estimate the cost of shooting per day and produce a provisional budget estimating the total amount of funding required. Once the producer, on their own or with the backing of financiers, mobilises the required amount, the movie proceeds into the official pre-production stage.

In the pre-production stage of the movie, the line producer shoulders the responsibility of ensuring there is a clear channel of communication between the direction team and the production team. The direction team is comprised of the director, associate director and assistant directors. The production team comprises heads of different departments like lighting, transport, art and set design. A clear channel of communication is vital between these departments in order to ensure that a shoot date is set and schedules are adhered to. Often it looks like a line producer is superhuman because of the range of responsibilities and duties that are part of their portfolio. But that is the where the difference matters between a good line producer and a not-so-good line producer. Whether the content works with audiences or not is for the judgement of another time, but whether the production house has done a good job or not depends to a large extent on the line producer. Though the buck stops with the producer, in most cases the line producer is the last one to decide whether to pass the buck to the producer or not. This is because the line producer manages or oversees all pre-production activities like the smooth functioning of the production office; zeroing in on apt locations; securing all necessary permissions; ensuring that paperwork is in place including insurance and health and safety requirements; keeping an eye out on all the union requirements to avoid violation notices; and finding the right suppliers for equipment, junior artists and for set design.

When actual production commences, the efforts taken in the pre-production phase ensure that the production runs smoothly and progresses well. However, if planning is haphazard there will be a significant impact on the pace of production, adversely affecting the completion schedule and adding escalating costs. Therefore, the line producer has to be vigilant to ensure that crises are avoided and that the production runs unhampered. In the Indian movie industry, there are veteran line producers with a large repertoire of knowledge and experience who have weathered many storms to ensure a movie stays on schedule. Though every line producer has an allowance that enables them to factor in an escalation of costs up to 10 per cent, it is a joint decision for the producer and director whether to make certain changes to cast and crew or shoot in a different location. Such changes might be due to lack of desired quality in completed footage, making a re-shoot inevitable, incurring a budget escalation of more than the 10 per cent contingency buffer that a line producer can apply at their discretion. In the Indian cinema industry, superstition, religious beliefs and traditions go hand in hand, therefore a movie commences shooting with the breaking of a coconut to appease the Gods and to seek blessings. When the movie concludes shooting, a pumpkin is broken to ward off evil spirits so that the movie can proceed smoothly into post-production and release. The line producer is the decision-maker for commencing and concluding principal photography by deciding on good days on which to break coconuts and pumpkins.

Assessing the skills and qualifications required for the challenging role of line producer is a difficult task because it is a role traditionally learnt on the job. Though movie schools tend to offer short courses for training line producers, no amount of theory can be substituted for solid practical experience. One producer with 22 years' experience as a line producer sums it up:

> Every day is an experience, and learning from mistakes happens regularly, but learning means correctly learning from the production. When I was with a producer, it is the real learning for me, of course, it might sound like a very old formula, but that was the real learning it was the golden formula and success formula.

It is an unwritten rule that a good line producer has good experience with different production houses and different genres of movies. Modern-day production houses tend to hire business school graduates who are well-versed in scheduling and budgets. They become part of the production team and get to learn the technical processes of moviemaking on the job. The most important skill a line producer needs is networking and developing a solid database of industry contacts. Contacts and experience are the two assets of a line producer that command respect from the production crew. It also helps if a line producer is good at disaster management, since movie production is a veritable minefield of disasters waiting to happen. A relatively young producer, who has moved up the ranks from film school to line producer to executive producer and then producer, summed it up:

> As an EP (executive producer), or LP (line producer) if you have one film or two film experiences that is more than enough according to me. If you have a course or if you did some diploma or degree or whatever, definitely it will help in setting the budget, streamlining the project and having transparency. Here transparency is zero, on the daily basis we can see the cost and monitor the cost, once we get into the flow of production on the third day and later the cost will start rising. If we have the experience, then we can steer it onto the track and ensure that there is no cost over-run. If we have a right model, we can monitor and cut down.

One of the best pieces of advice that Rajeev received was from a line producer who advised him, since the author and the production house were new to production, to be prepared for the unexpected and to be adept at crisis management. In film production, crises come in multiples rather than singly, even before one gets a chance to take a deep breath after coming out of one crisis, the next will be ready and waiting for immediate attention. This was valuable advice and summed up the sensitive role played by a line producer. The sensitivity stems from the fact that the line producer is always at the coalface and will bear the brunt of the problems. A good line producer shields the producer from many of these problems.

Executive producer

In the Indian movie industry, the title and role of an executive producer are not clearly defined because the industry did not evolve as one large production house simultaneously managing multiple movie productions. Most independent movie producers in Indian cinema work on one project at a time, or in some cases two projects concurrently, but no more than that. This is due to several factors like poor funding, lack of a big studio concept or setup, or the inability of independent producers to expand and branch out due to the risk-averse nature of the movie process. For some projects, an executive producer is hired because of multiple projects and business ventures operating simultaneously, resulting in congestion among the top management. The specific role assigned to the executive producer is to be the representative of the producer on set and during the shooting and production of the movie. In other cases, the financiers, or the studio bankrolling the project, can appoint an executive producer to keep an eye on production to ensure that their investment is not at risk.

There are several examples of executive producers being former producers or of being a producer who wants to partner with the current production to provide management support to the main producer to ensure that the movie is completed on time, within budget and to a high standard of artistry and creativity. The executive producer can also be a major investor in the project or hold stakes in the creative content of the movie in production. As a rule of thumb, executive producers do not involve themselves in the technical details of the moviemaking process. A second-generation producer, who has trained his daughter into the intricacies of production, comments:

> I would say that a training for a producer will come only from a being a line producer and executive producer. If you notice all the big producers of yesteryear, barring the second generation of studio owners, these are all people who have started their career as line producers or executive producers and grew into the role of independent producers, so they know how to handle production. Now studio owners have also at some time seen

this and they have hired executive producers who have become producers and they have children who continue production on that banner.

We often notice leading stars like Matt Damon or leading directors like Steven Spielberg getting a title credit as executive producer; apart from the practical roles and duties mentioned, it can also be a good ploy for marketing and the business development of a movie. A movie can have more than one executive producer depending on the specific role or expertise they bring in. An executive producer should be someone who adds value to the project rather than being a dead weight. They should bring their skills to the project: negotiation skills for striking deals, or bringing distribution and exhibition muscle to the project.

Conclusion

The movie industry portrays an image of glitz, glamour and luxurious lifestyles. Surely for an industry that has a less than 20 per cent success rate, it cannot all be so positive! The low success rate in the movie industry points to the high risks involved and also places it in the same bracket as other entrepreneurial ventures that have a similar chance of succeeding or failing. The biggest risk-taker, with everything to lose if a movie fails at the box office, is the producer. Unfortunately, the producer has the image of being a money bag whose sole purpose is paying the bills while everyone else is involved in the creative process. This is a stereotypical misrepresentation that has been in vogue for years, mainly due to the new entrants coming into the business who have limited or no skills in production and are solely enamoured of the supposed glitz and glamour. Movie schools have introduced production courses, but enrolment is much lower compared to other technical and artistic courses. Unfortunately, there is a belief that aspiring producers must have expertise because they have access to funds, which is a high-risk belief. Production is not just about money. Movie production is an amalgamation of creativity, prudent financial planning, project management, marketing campaigns and ingenuity in distribution. Surely one person cannot be blessed with all these talents, so it is imperative that certain abilities have to be acquired with experience and learning over a period of time. There are producers who are tight-fisted and ensure that their movies never go over budget and never attempt lavish productions. There are producers who are marketing geniuses at selling their own movies. There are producers who have the ability to judge and choose a script that taps into the pulse of audiences. A producer who can combine all of the above will have a high chance of success and, if a movie fails, it is safe to assume that the producer had failed on one or two of these vital aspects of the role. Controlling every moving part of the movie's production is the main role of a producer. Though all the other critical players can function independently without connection to the others, a producer's role is to connect all the dots so that the end result is good and wins audience approval.

The business of movies is a business of teamwork and coordination. If one link of the team underperforms, the entire product is weakened, leading inevitably to sub-optimal results. This chapter showcased the themes that emerged from conversations with Indian movie stakeholders and also the importance and interconnectedness of all the players in their quest to deliver good movies on both the artistic and commercial fronts.

References

Aldrich, H and Ruef, M 2017, 'Unicorns, gazelles, and other distractions on the way to understanding real entrepreneurship in America', *Academy of Management Perspectives*, vol. 32, no. 4, pp. 458–472.

Audretsch, D, Mason, C, Miles, MP and O'Connor, A 2018, 'The dynamics of entrepreneurial ecosystems', *Entrepreneurship and Regional Development*, vol. 30, no. 3–4, pp. 471–474.

Erigha, M 2015, 'Race, gender, Hollywood: Representation in cultural production and digital media's potential for change', *Sociology Compass*, vol. 9, pp. 78–89.

Fisher, R, Merlot, E and Johnson, LW 2018, 'The obsessive and harmonious nature of entrepreneurial passion', *International Journal of Entrepreneurial Behaviour and Research*, vol. 24, no. 1, pp. 22–40.

Friedland, R and Mohr, J 2004, 'The cultural turn in American sociology', in R Friedland and J Mohr (eds), *Matters of Culture: Cultural Sociology in Practice*, pp. 1–69, Cambridge University Press, Cambridge.

Gioia, DA and Chittipeddi, K 1991, 'Sensemaking and sensegiving in strategic change initiation', *Strategic Management Journal*, vol. 12, pp. 433–448.

Isenberg, D 2010, 'The Big Idea: How to Start an Entrepreneurial Revolution', *Harvard Business Review*, vol. 88, no. 6, pp. 41–50.

Lauzen, MM 2019, 'The celluloid ceiling: Behind the scenes employment of women on the top 100, 250 and 500 films of 2018', *Center for the Study of Women in Television and Film*. San Diego, CA.

Lounsbury, M and Glynn, MA 2001, 'Cultural entrepreneurship: Stories, legitimacy, and the acquisition of resources', *Strategic Management Journal*, vol. 22, no. 6, pp. 545–564.

Lounsbury, M and Glynn, MA 2019, *Cultural Entrepreneurship: A New Agenda for the Study of Entrepreneurial Processes and Possibilities*, Cambridge University Press, New York.

Moody, P 2017, 'US embassy support for Hollywood's global dominance: Cultural imperialism redux', *International Journal of Communication*, vol. 11, pp. 2912–2925.

Mota, A, Braga, V and Ratten, V 2019, 'Entrepreneurship motivation: Opportunity and necessity', in V Ratten, P Jones, V Braga and C Marques (eds), *Sustainable Entrepreneurship: Contributions to Management Science*, pp. 139–165, Springer, New York.

O' Connor, A, Stam, E, Sussan, F and Audretsch, D 2018, '*Entrepreneurial Ecosystems: Place Based Transformations and Transitions*', Springer, Switzerland.

Obodaru, O 2012, 'The self not taken: How alternative selves develop and how they influence our professional lives', *Academy of Management Review*, vol. 37, no. 1, pp. 34–57.

Sarma, S and Sunny, SA 2017, 'Civic entrepreneurial ecosystems: Smart city emergence in Kansas City', *Business Horizons*, vol. 60, no. 6, pp. 843–853.

Shane, S 2003, *A General Theory of Entrepreneurship: The Individual—Opportunity Nexus*, Edward Elgar, Cheltenham.

Spigel, B 2017, 'The relational organization of entrepreneurial ecosystems', *Entrepreneurship Theory and Practice*, vol. 41, no. 1, pp. 49–72.

Timmons, JA, Muzyka, DF, Stevenson, HH and Bygrave, WD 1987, 'Opportunity recognition: The core of entrepreneurship', in NC Churchill *et al.* (ed), *Frontiers of Entrepreneurship Research*, pp. 109–123, Babson College, Wellesley, MA.

Vallerand, RJ 2015, *The Psychology of Passion: A Dualistic Model*, Oxford University Press, New York.

Vallerand, RJ, Blanchard, CM, Genevieve, AK, Ratelle, R, Leonard, C, Gagne, M and Josee, MM 2003, 'Les passions de l'ame: One obsessive and harmonious passion', *Journal of Personality and Social Psychology*, vol. 85, no. 4, pp. 756–767.

Van der Zwan, P, Thurik, R, Verheul, I and Hessels, J 2016, 'Factors influencing the entrepreneurial engagement of opportunity and necessity entrepreneurs', *Eurasian Business Review*, vol. 6, no. 3, pp. 273–295.

Venkataraman, S 1997, 'The distinctive domain of entrepreneurship research: An editor's perspective', in JA Katz (ed), *Advances in Entrepreneurship, Firm Emergence and Growth*, vol. 3, pp. 119–138, JAI Press, Greenwich, CT.

4

GREEN-LIGHTING
Resourcing movies in India

To make a great movie you need three things—the script, the script and the script.
Alfred Hitchcock, arguably the all-time best thriller director

Difference between predator and prey in a business ecosystem is determined by the strength of one's next idea.
Ronnie Screwvala, Founder, UTV and RSVP

Introduction

One of the ironies of the movie industry is that British-born Alfred Hitchcock thrived in the US movie business as a producer and director but never won an Academy Award. Though some of his movies won the coveted Best Picture award, he never won the Best Director award. The Academy possibly realised its error and awarded a Thalberg Memorial Award to Hitchcock towards the end of his career. Is there any particular reason he was overlooked? It is a matter for debate, as there is no authoritative source to explain, or any official information from the Academy itself. It can be assumed that the Academy does not consider thrillers to be serious cinema and therefore Hitchcock, who dedicated his life to making thrillers, missed out. Who decides that thrillers are inferior to serious cinema? Certainly not the audience who buy the tickets. It might be the intellectuals who aspire for cinema to be valued as a serious art form. Therein lies the rub. Where is the rule saying that an art form should not entertain? Cinema is primarily a source of entertainment and the audience expect to be transported to a different world—entertained, stimulated and forgetting all their worries for 120 to 180 minutes inside a theatre. The case is similar for Indian movies. Their failure to win Academy Awards is due to their propensity to cater to those who want popular entertainment.

Green-lighting

In an economically developing country like India, cinema is the cheapest form of entertainment, with tickets costing less than US$2 in many cities across the country. Movie producers are guided by the craving for entertainment and ensure that a majority of the movies entertain rather than educate. However, there are odd exceptions that are quickly classified as art cinema and enjoy only a tiny fraction of the business pie. As one second-generation producer who has occupied influential positions in the leading movie trade associations in India commented:

> A movie is the cheapest form of entertainment in India; for 100 bucks (USD$1.5) you can go around the world, dream and come back. It is not just two and a half hours. I see it as more than 15 hours: you start thinking about it when you buy the movie ticket; you think about it when you get into the car; you think about it when you reach the theatre. After you come back, you think about it for another three or four hours. Every time you think about it, it is 15 to 20 hours of entertainment.

With everything riding on entertainment, the process of approving the right script—called green-lighting—assumes inordinate significance. The process of choosing the right script is one of many risky decisions for the entrepreneurial producer.

It is impossible to decipher a scientific formula for understanding the entrepreneurial process of approving a script. Guesswork tends to dominate the process, with expert opinion and intuition thrown into the mix. Hence, the risk is huge. If there were a scientific formula that guaranteed success, then there would not be such a high percentage of failures in the movie industry. One successful producer with a professional background who has analysed the moviemaking process in USA compared to India, recounts his experience of learning the ropes of green-lighting.

> In India, producers come to directors and narrate a story. That was a big leap of faith. The movie industry did not have a script at that time. It seemed like a poor way to convince me to produce a movie. It was too much of a leap of faith for me to believe in the narrator's dreams. Then I realised that there is something called as a script. There is something called a screenplay. So, I went back and learnt about them, read books and went for screenwriting workshops, I said OK, fine, a movie can be visualised on paper. I developed the skill of seeing the movie on paper, as a producer. We see it on paper, read it and visualise it.

> There is a high chance of movies failing in the industry. A very high chance. These were the two biggest points that I realised. The first one was script. They use a narration which is a bad tool that leads to more failures and you are never able to track somebody's vision.
>
> Then, we were expecting two big skill sets from the same person: directing and writing. That's another stark contrast that I found between Hollywood movies and, you know, movies that are being done in India. In Hollywood the writers are different: the process was that somebody found interesting written material and the production houses procured it and then they found the appropriate director to execute the project.

Remarks from the producer's story indicate the effort required to break behavioural norms. A project in the Indian movie industry typically commences with a one-line narration. Eighty per cent of the scripts in India are knocked back at the one-line stage. Therefore, the person pitching for the project—in many cases an aspiring director—has to tempt the producer by the novelty of his vision and attract him with that one line. As a leading financier aptly put it, directors try to lure producers into production by promising them 'multi-fold returns on their investment'. From the producers' point of view, the product needs to be sold well and, with past success as an indicator for future success, they green-light the project. For example, as one producer mentioned, the must-have flavour of a particular year was low-budget movies, so when the director approached the producer with a low-budget script, the producer said: 'Let's go ahead as the risk is limited. If the movie is successful, we will make a lot of money. If it fails, the loss will not be significant.'

Decisions are made with the business potential of that one-line story hook in mind. To gain a better understanding of this scenario, keep in mind that every one-line pitcher is scouting around for their source of employment for the next 12 to 14 months, so they are selling not just the project but also themselves and their viability for handling the project. Producers are used to listening to pitches that are sometimes dead boring but at other times riveting and attention-grabbing. For example, one director once narrated a three-generation family story for five hours—including every aspect of set design, plot points and emotional highlights—in a spellbinding manner.

The producer and his team could not commit to the project due to budgetary constraints and limited access to stars. But they predicted that it could be a blockbuster. The prediction proved to be right. That movie turned out to be one of the all-time hits of the Indian movie industry. So the point to be taken is: if the producer prefers a narrative over a read-through of the full script, it is better to narrate for three to four hours rather than give a one-line narration. As one experienced producer who had produced 14 movies commented on a movie: 'Though the narration was very good, we could not visualise the success of the movie, so we did not commit to the budget. Thus, we did not green-light the project, sadly. That movie went on to become a blockbuster.'

The approach to green-lighting a project with one-liners prompts the narrator to choose the main plot point and explain it succinctly. However, a movie has to hold the audience's attention for more than 100 minutes. The one-line aspect can lose its appeal when it becomes part of the broader story. The majority of producers move into production mode after green-lighting a project based on that one line. They use it to hook star, cast and crew for the project. Story development takes place in parallel with the pre-production phase and script improvement is often ongoing, even on-set, while shooting. In many ways, this is a recipe for disaster since the project loses direction and starts floundering. Creative improvisation on the script is always welcome but having no script is like a rudderless ship. Risk escalates. In retrospect, this would mean that green-lighting such a project was a bad decision.

Predicting the success of a movie is not easy or simple. However, the examples above offer a glimpse into the thought process of the producer, and the approach to selling of the director, with the weak points of the script identified during narration. What, then, are the typical pathways for producers in the Indian movie industry to green-light projects?

Pathway 1: Acquire the remake rights of a successful movie in a different language. Assign a writer, or team of writers, to adapt this successful story into the native milieu for which it is being remade. This will ensure the producer has identified a successful formula that worked in a different market and all that needs to be done is to replicate the formula, albeit with some modifications for local preferences, for there to be a high chance of success. There was one late producer in the Indian movie industry who was an expert in this remake formula; all of his movies were remakes. His son's remarks follow.

My father was very successful, I am not aware of any other production house that made successful remakes. My father made only remakes. He had a golden run of successes. There are certain subjects that work in every language and are universal. My father never thought of an original idea at any given time. He said that he likes to keep this going as long as he can but at the same time, those days there was no Google and no checking on what is going on. So, he would take a flight to Bombay sit in the taxi, ask the taxi driver what the good movies are, and the taxi driver will take him to the hit movies. He bought a ticket for him and the taxi driver, go sit and watch it with him. He will just watch for the reaction of the audience and try to understand if it will work in other languages. If he likes the movie, he will watch the night show again. He will watch the matinee with the taxi driver and the night show alone and watch it again to see if the reactions are consistent. Especially where the applause and appreciation are and where the audience is restless.

Next day morning he will meet the producer and sit in his office and tell the yarn that he has come from down south and it is a small market there. He will buy the rights, in all languages. He was a very good negotiator. He used to be very hard on prices but the fairest paymaster. Being an actor, he knew how to handle actors and manage their expectations. He had the natural instinct to pick up subjects and judge from audience reactions, many people have tried remakes and not succeeded.

My father used to buy the scripts from the original. He used to purchase the stock shots that were useful and could be replicated. He will buy the music track separately if it is difficult for our guys to recreate it. He will do all that, come here and change the comedy track. He will always have one lady comedian as a permanent artist in his movies. He would make the male comedian character the female comedian character but keep the same comic element. It worked for him.

Pathway 2: This pathway is straightforward. It simply adapts existing product to the screen with the highest bidder obtaining the rights to the movie adaptation. For example, the producer may acquire the rights for a successful play, such as *West Side Story* or *Fiddler on the Roof* and adapt it to the screen. This pathway was a template developed by Hollywood during its formative years. The most successful movies were adaptations of either Broadway hits or highly popular works of literature. Once the rights are acquired, the producer allots the work to different writers to come up with a suitable screen adaptation. Producer and director decide on the best version and start shooting it for the screen. Even good screen adaptations tend to get passed around different production houses due to the lack of confidence of the producer.

Pathway 3: This pathway is a complete green-field project where the writer picks up a social issue and weaves a plot around it. For example, one leading producer produced more than 30 movies. The producer said:

> I was inspired by the story of the Chief Minister's wife going to university with her son when she was in her 50s. I liked that story and wanted to make it into a commercially viable movie. I contracted two screen writers to write the story. I created a role for the movie where the leading protagonist is the father who goes to school with his son. It was a novel concept as a 60-year-old actor played that role. It became a blockbuster.

The runaway success of the movie was due to its fresh concept. As an entrepreneur, the producer recognised that going to university later in life struck a chord among the audience, as it was a novel idea. This notion was only just beginning to be taken up by Indian people to whom education is a key path to change their lives for themselves and or their children.

Many great science-fiction movies like *Star Wars* were conceived and developed in this manner. Stripped down to its bare level, *Star Wars* is a simple story of a fight between good and bad and the power of evil to convert one of the good guys. This simple story would not have been green-lit in single-line narration because the richness of the setting and characters cannot be explained in such a short form. If ever there were a strong case for reading a full script, it is *Star Wars*. Forty years later, we agree that *Star Wars* created movie magic and history, but in the early 1970s, studio executives had difficulty understanding or visualising the grandeur and scale of that production. Naturally, this script was tossed and turned around between several studios before 20th Century Fox agreed to green-light it. Similarly, in the Indian movie industry, there are several examples of scripts that were turned down by production houses and leading stars because they could not visualise the script on the screen.

Pathway 4: This pathway entails banking on the past track record of the director. If the director has just delivered a blockbuster and is in the market for a producer who can mount their next directorial venture, then many producers may green-light a project without even listening to the pitch. This is because they are relying on past performance as the predictor of future success. One young producer had produced several blockbuster movies up to this time. He used this pathway a lot for green-lighting movies. He remarked:

> We chased the director who gave the market three consecutive super hits. At this point, you don't ask for the script. It depends on the director's judgement to deliver a successful product. We missed the target, so the content that was developed was more on the comic side rather than the hero's core strengths of action and emotions. The movie was delivered in not so great a way. We watched the movie before it was released. We made a few corrections, edited the footage, but still the core content was focusing on the sidekick rather than the hero. When the audience comes to watch a movie, they come to watch the hero and not the sidekick. Since the director has worked with the sidekick for his last three movies and delivered hits, the lines and the roles were slightly lopsided towards the sidekick. That proved fatal to the project.

In entrepreneurship, past performance may not be a safe predictor of future success. Every individual project requires individual attention in order to avoid the kind of mistakes that were made in the last example. The producer wanted to cash in on the popularity of the director. There no shortcuts when green-lighting a movie project, as this resulting flop illustrates. Even in entrepreneurial ventures, risk needs to be carefully evaluated.

These four pathways are the most popular for green-lighting projects. After green-lighting and producing the movie, if the movie is a success, Indian movie producers have the ability to squeeze every last rupee out of it. Due to the geographical vastness of India and the multilingual audiences, as described in Chapter 2, the Indian movie landscape offers many avenues for remakes and dubbing into other languages. It is on record that a very successful movie named *Pasamalar* (*The Flower of Love*) was remade in ten other languages and was successful in all of them. Though there are different pathways that producers can follow to green-light a movie, the main justification for green-lighting (or not) lies in the perceived business potential. In other words, does the movie have the potential to be commercially viable?

Business Potential: In common business parlance, breaking even is the most critical aspect of any business. The viability of a venture depends on whether it can break even and recover the initial investment. The business potential and chance of breaking even weigh on the minds of the movie producers while green-lighting or not green-lighting a project. There are some successful producers who have the uncanny knack of sensing the business potential of a project from just the one-line narration. However, such producers are in a very small minority. The challenge confronting a producer while green-lighting a project is that they need to weigh up the total costs that an approved script will incur and compare them with the earning potential of the project. If the earnings are not commensurate with the expected spending, then the project will not be green-lit. As mentioned earlier, there is no scientific formula and this works on the basis of the producer's intuition and feedback from the distributor and exhibitors, who are adept at pegging the commercial value of a movie based on its script premise, genre and star cast.

Producers, however, do not want business success alone; they want artistic success too. They sometimes green-light, even when they are aware that the project might not make money, because they have other aspirations, such as winning an award or a special commendation. As one producer who won the President of India's Gold Medal commented:

> As a producer, I have made many movies and not all of them for the commercial mainstream. One of our movies was positioned for the art film festival circuit and had a clear aim of winning the President of India's medal.

Producers who build a project solely around a star are doing it for commercial reasons and not for artistic reasons. There have been many instances when a project was green-lit without even a script, simply for the reason that a leading star and leading director were available and willing to work together. Stars know their power. One senior producer who changed three directors on the demand of the star, commented: 'The stars are aware that we producers are at their mercy, so they make unreasonable demands.'

When this happens, a script is developed based on the combination of star and director and their business potential. Furthermore, a star cast used to be the all-consuming fixation in the earlier days of the movie business. Many productions in the Indian movie industry kept stars under contract to the production houses, and scripts were green-lit with the box office potential and the images of the contracted stars in mind. Though stars are no longer contracted for long periods to production houses, it is the box office potential of the stars that determines the commercial viability and the green-lighting of projects. The leading stars, the director and the music director—in that order—are generally the magnets around which the business potential is centred. The 'combination craze' is explained in detail in Chapter 5. In these scenarios, the main reason for green-lighting a project is the business potential of the project.

Resourcing

Looking at the key players in movie production, we can appreciate the rationale for pooling talent and infrastructure behind a movie industry gravitating towards an ecosystem. In the movie production ecosystem, the nine main players—apart from the producers—are: directors, financiers, main technical crew, additional crew, cast, studio, marketing team, distributors and exhibitors. These nine key players can be grouped under the four broad categories of financiers, exhibitors, cast and crew. Each of these categories is now discussed in relation to the role of the entrepreneurial producer and their circle, then examined thematically.

Financiers

Financiers generally tend to operate behind the scenes, provide funding to a particular project or a slate of projects. They are not involved in the creative process but only in the commercial aspect of harvesting the venture. Financiers have enough clout to alter the release schedule—and sometimes the cast—according to commercial demands. In the Indian movie industry, for many years the financiers were unorganised and operated without proper documentation, with everything based on handshake agreements. The value system was different in the earlier era, and the producers and financiers had a very healthy and mutually respectful relationship. However, with affluence and changes in the social fabric, the value system also changed and, today, all financiers operate with clear documentation and within the legal framework. In the 1980s, movie financing was viewed with suspicion due to rumours that funds were coming in from underworld activities and unaccounted sources. However, with proactive clamping down by the government and strict self-regulation and monitoring by the industry, movie financing has streamlined itself and operates as a non-banking financial sector (NBFC). However, market economics and demand for finance from the movie industry ensure that the rate of interest charged is very high: at times climbing to 48 per cent per annum. However, the majority of funding is in the range of 18 to 24 per cent—still high compared to other sectors but in the context of uncertainty, and given the failure rate, it is deemed to be justified.

The relationship between financier and producer tends to vary from cordial to contentious. A glimpse into a cordial relationship is offered by one producer:

> One day, a leading financier commented that he had witnessed producers purchasing properties in wives and children's names to avoid paying financiers. They claim to have lost money on the movie and had sundry reasons for requesting interest rate reductions. I never asked any financier to reduce interest or reduce the principal amount for me. I sold my properties and cleared my outstanding debts with two leading financiers.

When a producer depends on the financier for the funding to launch a project, the relationship ought to be one of mutual trust and respect. The producer needs the financier for securing funds for a new project, whereas the financier needs the interest accrual from the producer in order for the financing business to grow in a profitable manner. This can be seen in the remarks of a producer who failed and started again:

> How did I come back from failure? I started from scratch. I had to start with nothing. That was my strength. I used to go and meet people who lent me money; in fact, I used to meet them almost on a daily basis and tell them about my plans. Instead of running away from them and not answering their calls, I made it a point to take them into my confidence and assure them that I am working towards coming out from this big setback. They believed me, seeing my commitment, dedication and focus. I told them that without their support I cannot come back. They agreed to support me.

Similarly, another producer who experienced losses remarks on the vital support provided by financiers in times of crisis:

> Financially it was a big loss. Thankfully we had financiers who supported us at that point in time. We had income tax issues. We had an income tax raid two days before the release of the movie. Our financiers supported us really well; they were very supportive from all angles. They did not pressurise us for the release funds. That was a very big support at that time.

The financier is a key member of the producer's team and inner circle. One respected financier who works in a corporate setup explained the difficulties of obtaining finance in the 1980s and 1990s when movie producers were considered 'unprofessional players'. For example, the movie industry was operating on a cash basis in a parallel economy. He shared this with us:

> Initially it was about lending. We found an opportunity for professional lending. Because of the Reserve Bank of India (RBI) notification, the banks would not lend for movie production. They are not supposed to because, as an industry, the RBI decided not to lend and not to let the banks lend, so the banks never used to touch movies. What happened was that all the unprofessional players came into the industry. It was a cash business. Part of the movie culture was about cash, so there were guys who were lending cash and collecting cash, so there was a gap there for professional lending. The learning in that business was that you should not get too greedy about growth in an industry. If you are the largest lender, given the success rates of movies, you will end up being the person with the maximum outstanding amount to be recovered.

Despite these difficulties for movie producers in India, this financier found a way to 'connect' with the business and keep a 'tight leash' on managing funds as well as learning to judge which movies were going go to be successful in order to safeguard his investment. In other words, he gained a 'ringside view' of the industry that enabled him to support the producers. This financier shared with us the importance of having a helicopter view of the industry, which is denied to producers because they are too close to their productions:

> In the movie business, where you don't even know how the funds are going to be used, I was able to connect, closely monitor and keep a tight leash on progress, use of funds, etc. It was successful. The other aspect is to understand which genres do well, and who has the right combination of technicians and actors; what kinds of budgets do well. It gave me a ringside view of the industry because as a producer, you get tied to your project, and focused on it. At best you get access to three or four newer prospective opportunities where they narrate stories. Some stars meet you. But your exposure is limited. However, as a lender, I had great exposure to the industry. In the time that it takes to produce one movie, I lent to ten movies. I evaluated another 20 movies. That gave me tremendous visibility of what was going on and tracking it was great learning for both industry and trade.

Learning from the industry and understanding the trade is essential for both producers and financiers because both of them need to have their finger on the pulse so that risk is mitigated. Many independent producers feel there is a higher proportion of risk when associating with private financiers, so they prefer to work with a bank or a studio. In the Indian market, due to the stringent conditions imposed by the Reserve Bank, banks are wary of the movie industry and rarely venture into financing movies. This leaves producers with limited options. As one producer who worked with a corporate multi-national before branching out on his own commented: 'Working with this multi-national helped me understand the intricacies of funding a project and imbibing a professional culture in financing and executing a project as opposed to dealing with independent financiers.'

In other words, the only other option is to approach a professional studio like Disney, Fox or Viacom to finance their next movie project.

The Studio: The studio is essential to movie production: it provides the equipment, the lots and the processing space for making movies. In many instances, the studio can itself be a producer or a financial backer. If a large studio decides to back a project, the job of a producer becomes easier because they do not need to worry about showcasing and revenue-recovery for the project. In the Indian movie industry, the studios in the earlier years operated under the 'first copy' agreement. Under this agreement, the studio and the independent producer agree on a set amount as the cost of the movie and studio will finance the movie up to that amount. Once the movie is completed, the studio takes over to market, distribute and exhibit the movie. This way, neither the producer nor the studio are stretching their bandwidth, and they are able to focus on the areas of their expertise. A producer's strength and expertise lies in assembling a good cast and crew and executing a project, whereas a studio's strength lies in marketing and providing wide marketing of the movie. The three major Hollywood studios mentioned above have established their presence in the Indian market by following this template. After getting a foothold on the market and gaining first-hand knowledge of the tricky terrain of Indian cinema, these studios spread their wings and began launching projects on their own. Additionally, the studios have access to, or run, well-established distribution networks, which ensures that the producer does not end up in a situation where the movie is good but, due to bad showcasing, it does not garner good revenues. This brings us to the last critical player in the Indian cinematic landscape.

Exhibitors

As reflected in the name, an exhibitor is a person who exhibits the movie on a screen. Traditionally, it was only the screens and theatres that exhibited the movie, but over time VHS, DVD, satellite, digital and direct-to-home streaming have all taken up prominent slices of the exhibition pie. Gone are the days when a patron could only watch a movie in theatres. Now, if they miss it on the big screen, they have several small-screen options. Before getting into the exhibition stage, there is one very important link in the whole puzzle: a link that acts as a buffer between the producer and the end viewer. This is the distributor and we will consider them here before moving back to exhibitors.

Distributors: Distributors pick up the rights to distribute a movie in a particular territory. These rights are normally assigned for a specific period of time, like three or five years. During that period, the distributor can screen that particular movie as many times and on as many screens as they wish. There are typically three types of distribution arrangements that a producer and a distributor can enter into:

(a) Plain Distribution arrangement where the distributor circulates the movie in a territory and charges a commission of 10 to 20 per cent on the net of tax revenue, deducts this amount and remits the balance to the producer.

(b) Outright Purchase where the distributor purchases the rights of the movie for a stipulated period of time and pays an agreed amount to the producer. In that timeframe, if the movie collects more than the paid amount, the producer does not have any claim on that extra amount, which istermed the 'overflow' amount in cinema jargon. Similarly, if the movie collects less than the agreed amount, the distributor does not have any right to claim a refund for the losses sustained.

(c) Minimum Guarantee (MG) arrangement, where the distributor is willing to take a portion of the risk and pays a minimum sum that is non-refundable by the producer. If the movie collects more than this minimum amount, then the overflow amount is shared between the distributor and the producer in a pre-agreed percentage split. As one very successful low-budget movie producer commented: 'All the distributors on the first day of principal photography used to hand over advance money and book the movie for exhibition in their areas. That concept is gone now. Today, no distributor buys the movie even after it is complete and ready for release. They all look to release the movie and then pay after the audience has watched the movie. That minimum guarantee is not available'.

The final link in this labyrinth of movie production is the exhibitor. The exhibitor screens the movie in cinemas owned, operated or leased by them. For the privilege of showcasing a movie, an exhibitor charges commission from the movie's distributors. As a general rule of thumb this is 50 per cent in the first week, 60 per cent in the second week and 70 per cent in the third week of a movie's box office collections during the run. This commission, as well as the revenue generated from advertising, parking, beverages and confectionery, becomes income for the exhibitors for building, operating, maintaining and upgrading their screens.

These days, a further final link has been added: that of the DVD and digital rights holders. A producer, for a monetary consideration, assigns the digital rights of a movie for a specified timeframe, or sometimes in perpetuity, to a consolidated digital rights acquirer. They in turn sell to the different TV channels around the world, as well as airlines and hotel networks. One producer goes as far as saying that the movie industry is growing and not shrinking because of the advent of multiple channels for exhibiting:

> The movie industry continued to grow when it should have shrunk. Thanks to the satellite business, television channels were vying with each other, so they were upping the price, and that has continued now because of Amazon Prime and Netflix. Those guys are keen because any new player wants to build a catalogue; they are coming and giving fancy numbers and thanks to that the industry is losing sight of budgets versus recoveries. Whenever new investors or a new group of funds come into the industry, the industry goes down. We can see it. Basically, lots of projects that should not be launched are launched. Then you see the struggle.

The struggle in the industry is clear when producers lament the fact that those who have invested their last penny want to recover the amount by any means and, in desperation, they are willing to give away the rights forever. This is another peculiar feature of the Indian movie industry, where digital rights are assigned for perpetuity, thereby cutting off future revenue options. A senior producer who has taken a break from active production laments the lack of morality in the movie business, comparing India to Hollywood:

> There is no morality in the business anymore. Try to snatch as much as possible. This becomes a problem. The future lies in digital cinema, digital exploitation, several kinds of exploitation, and also bringing down the cost. That is the most important thing.
> The cost is very high. A bad movement started about 20 years ago. We used to sell all the by-products other than the theatrical release in one lump sum to one particular person. It was catastrophic. Likewise, other digital selling should be for a period of three or five years, as in Hollywood. We are not doing it here. It is a disadvantage for us. Producers have to be more careful. Some of my friends—old-time producers who produced good movies in the old days and experienced failure recently—realised their money by reselling satellite rights for a period of five or ten years so they could recover something rather than losing everything. I don't think that the model will change; this is the greatest drawback for us. The digital players are giving more options to producers, but even when Netflix comes into India, they feel that they can bargain the satellite rights for five years. But when a mediator tells them that we are selling for perpetual means, they will be tempted.

Fair dealing and bringing down the cost are the most important things to do. And it is the producer who can do that. This brings us back to the role of the producer, discussed in detail in Chapter 3. The producer is the financial muscle behind a movie; they bring in the funding and put together the project. In most cases, the financial risk is completely borne by the producer, though the risk can be mitigated by selling the exhibition and telecast rights. The producer is the fulcrum around which the entire production process is centred. Therefore, even though there are nine other critical players in the Indian cinematic landscape, the most critical player is the producer, and it is the producer who controls every moving part of the production, as well as overseeing the role of the cast, crew, financiers and exhibitors.

Cast

What is a movie without a hero and a heroine? Whether it is Mickey and Donald, Tom and Jerry, Humphrey Bogart and Lauren Bacall, Richard Burton and Elizabeth Taylor or Shahrukh Khan and Kajol, the leading artists carry the movie on their shoulders. They open movies by drawing large crowds and only then does the content in the movie take off. Both leading and supporting cast add value and appeal to a movie project. However, in a large market like India, there is a surprisingly limited talent pool that can attract audiences and make projects commercially viable. In the words of one successful male producer who trained in the USA and then returned to India to develop his movie career:

> Today insecurity is very high. The Indian movie industry caters to ten actors, ten male actors, ten female actors, and ten directors. So, the quantum of people who are successful in the industry is low. Because of the high rate of failure—90 per cent of the movies don't work—movie work breeds a very small pool of successful people. That is the scary part. Because India is a slightly bigger industry, the sheer numbers will be bigger, maybe ten times bigger than the USA. Instead of 100 people, there will be 1,000 successful people. Imagine across India there are only 1,000 people who are successful in movies.

So, taking risks to make a movie successful requires investment in stars. It is easy to take an idealistic stance, stating that a producer should not chase stars. But market economics force producers to go after bankable stars who can ensure that the movie has some interest from the audience. The presence of stars also helps with marketing. With the advent of multiple screen complexes with limited seating and an abundance of content, making a movie with a totally new cast is challenging. However, if the budget is kept strictly under control and the content is good, the digital revolution has ensured that there might be a second life possible for such content-driven movies previously forced out of the theatrical circuit. Unable to meet demand for higher remuneration from popular artists, producers are looking at alternative forms of content development and execution.

For decades, whether it was Hollywood or the Indian movie industry, star remuneration was a significant component of production expenses. A leading actor with many decades of stardom stated, in a forthright manner, that he personally needs '50 per cent of the budget of any movie for his compensation'. This meant that the leading artist wanted to lock in 50 percent of the cost as his remuneration and wanted to control 100 percent of content creation thereby reducing the role of a producer to a mere cashier with limited involvement. However, he is not taking a stake in the revenue side. From a pure business sense, this cannot work because all the risk is being carried by the producer with limited or zero control of many facets of production. However, this particular project went ahead because the market credibility of star power was seen as important for such an entrepreneurial venture. Credibility comes with big stars. Of course, the producer went through a harrowing experience to recover the investment but was aided by the fact that the star created a marketing frenzy and the distributors supported this star. In a nutshell, that is the power of the star or the star cast. Many producers share this experience, and in fact, many producers in the Indian movie industry are synonymous with certain leading stars. They are branded as belonging to one 'camp' or the other. A lot of producers make lofty claims that they do not chase stars, they create stars. As you can see, casting is vital for a movie project and in many instances the cast makes or breaks a movie.

Crew

Though not always in the limelight, the crew are very much part of the team. After finalising the cast or alongside finalising the cast, the crew are recruited and the director is the captain of the crew. Though the different crafts of moviemaking are mentioned in detail later in this chapter, we mention them briefly below.

Director: Creative minds that conceive the entire project. The moving images we watch on the silver screen are an interpretation of the director's vision of the movie project. Normally, a director walks away with both the bouquets and brickbats for a movie. The control and power that a successful director exerts are captured in the words of this young producer who branched out on his own after being a partner in earlier ventures and who is experienced in handling established directors:

> We thought getting into the hands of an experienced and informed director would be safe. We signed director A and director B. We did movie A and movie B. We struggled a lot. In the edit suite we realised that the

content was not working. We weren't in the habit of getting into the shoot and disturbing it. We trusted the director. We tried to do maximum corrections and better the product. But established directors are not comfortable if producers edit their content and they feel that their creative freedom is being curbed.

This is a trend that established directors across the world follow. They are clear that the decision on final output should be theirs alone. However, some powerful and successful producers like Darryl F Zanuck bucked this trend because the industry accepted them as masters at gauging the pulse of the audience, as well as possessing the ability to decipher which sequence needed to be edited to maintain the tempo of the movie.

Main technical crew: Imagine watching a movie with no sound, no music, no lighting—it would be a rather bland and unpleasant experience. The main technical crew, comprising music director, cinematographer and editor support the director's vision and enhance the visuals to create the right ambience and experience for the audience. Due to the lack of formal training for movie producers, most producers tend to learn on the job, and they learn from the technical crew. Generally, the technical crew have qualifications. The director of photography has a diploma or degree in photography, the editor will likely have a diploma and so they are better qualified than a producer who has no formal qualifications in his role. Therefore, it is common for producers to acknowledge the role played by technicians in teaching them the nuances of moviemaking. One producer remarked:

> I learnt from good people. I learnt from good producers. I learnt quite a lot from senior directors, I learnt from well-established directors, you know, these people who did classic movies. Some directors, some excellent cinematographers, I learnt from them. I used to sit along with my father-in-law who was an established and successful producer in the editing table. I also learnt from him, and my editors and that gave me a lot of confidence.

Additional crew: Director and main technical crew are ably supported and assisted by scriptwriters, lighting technicians, music conductors, art directors and sound engineers. Though these crafts tend to stay out of the limelight, they are crucial for a movie project to take off. In the movie business, the additional crew are referred to as the non-glamorous crew because they stay predominantly behind the scenes. Nevertheless, their role in shaping the destiny of a movie project cannot be discounted because a movie is ultimately shaped in the post-production phase. In this phase these additional crew members play a major role. The importance of additional crew and the respect they are due is reflected in the words of one of the top producers:

I pay well because I believe that technicians should be paid well. A producer can be cost-conscious and tight-fisted in controlling unnecessary expenditure but not in squeezing the technicians, because they are the life of the movie. I donated half a million rupees to the movie employees' federation because movie technicians should be encouraged and supported. If I hear that a movie mediator is struggling, then I give him a cheque for half a million rupees. It is my own money. It is to help him in time of financial need.

Though the additional crew are given recognition during the rolling credits at the end of the movie, they are rarely noticed. However, they play a vital role in ensuring that the project moves along without hindrance.

Marketing agency/team: Hype around a project is generated by the manner in which it is marketed and positioned. Though the producers used to carry this responsibility in the initial days, not all present-day producers are equipped with the skill set and ability to pull off successful marketing campaigns, especially with the ever-changing social media dynamics. Therefore, a good marketing agency/team has become integral to a movie project. There are occasions when the producer realises that the project that was conceived and developed did not turn as anticipated, and there is a strong chance that the audience might reject the movie. At such a juncture, marketing comes in handy to create the necessary hype and recover the costs before any negative word of mouth affects revenue. In the words of one producer who found himself in this predicament:

I spoke to my company. Let's invest that extra $150,000 in marketing the movie. Let's be aggressive and create massive hype; you know what, that movie got the biggest opening in the career for that particular hero, and even today, he has not got that opening. We made our money; we recovered our money, but no profit. Everyone in the industry was surprised. Fantastic opening and we sold theatricals; we sold satellite, we sold overseas. I spent US$4 million, and I got back US$4 million plus interest. I got back everything for the company. My board of directors was highly appreciative. The remake and dubbing rights I sold because the hype was so good that it could be sold.

Marketing is extremely crucial in the present-day context, and is an important cog in the movie release wheel. It is extremely rare to have sleeper hits now because of the rise of multiplexes and multiple screens replacing single screens across the world. This means the life span of a movie is very short. In that short span, a producer has to recover as much investment as possible, so the first and second weekends determine the range of success or failure of a movie. A good marketing agency/team ensures that the opening is good; following that the intrinsic quality of the movie ensures whether it will have a long run or short run.

The production journey

Conceiving, executing and launching a movie is a laborious process and there are several moving parts that need to fit into a cohesive plan, so that an entertaining and successful potboiler hits the screen. The producer, whether they are independent or a large corporation, is the life and the core of movie production. Though a movie is ultimately a director's vision, the director is like the captain of a team and the producer is the owner/manager/coach. Both roles are complementary and cannot survive without the other. The movie production journey is mapped out using a modified version of the model of entrepreneurship in Timmons et al. (1987) (see Figure 4.1). It shows the moviemaking opportunity in the three stages of pre-production, production and post-production, identifying where scripting, filming, marketing and directing occur. The producer, of course, pulls it all together.

The production timeline, its key roles and requirements, are outlined in Table 4.1. The three stages of the production process mentioned above: pre-production, production, post-production, plus the final phase—the release—are described.

The pre-production phase, illustrated in Figure 4.2, entails script selection. Script selection is the opportunity-recognition part of the entrepreneurial process.

Scenario 1: Initiative from producer. Scripts are called for, and several scripts are pitched to the producer. The producer and his/her team listen to the full

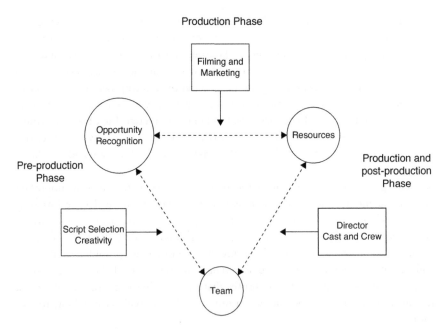

4.1   The movie production journey

TABLE 4.1 The production phases, milestones, roles and requirements

Production phase	Milestones	Roles and requirements
	Pre-production	
Pre-production Weeks 0–12	*Week 0*: Scripts are called for, pitched, assessed and approved; or a director or leading artist develops a script idea. *Week 1*: The producer identifies a director who can translate the script to screen. *Weeks 2–7*: Movie website launched and title announced. Co-branding opportunities identified and finalised. Production planning commences. *Weeks 8–12*: In-depth scheduling and planning to cost the production and establish logistics and contingencies.	There are 24 'crafts' of film-making: – Director – Cinematographer/Director of photography (DOP) – Movie editor – Composer/Director of music – Art director/Production designer – Casting agent for lead and supporting artists – Action/Stunt sequence coordinator – Script 'doctors'/writers – Voiceover artists – Line producer – Head of make-up – Costume designer – Still photographer – Marketing, publicity design and execution team – Lighting technicians – Sound/Audio recording and mixing team – Tradespeople – Production department assistants – Transportation and logistics – Outdoor unit technicians – Housekeeping – Agent for crowdsourcing – Choreographer/Background singers – Censor/Certification process coordinator
Production Weeks 13–24	– The 24 'crafts' of film-making are established. – Principal photography or the 'shooting' commences and concludes. – Most major productions can be shot in 90–120 days; this is an ideal time frame for the actual shooting to be wound up.	

(*Continued*)

TABLE 4.1 (Cont.)

Production phase	Milestones	Roles and requirements
	Pre-production	
Post-production **Weeks 25–52**	*Week 25*: Once shooting is completed, the first marketing collateral—a first look or digital poster—is released. With this release, movie marketing has officially begun. *Weeks 26–40*: Post-production activities like editing, dubbing, sound mixing, colour grading are completed. Producers exhibit a promotional reel to a test-marketing audience. *Weeks 41–52*: Movie release date is officially announced, and the marketing activities kick into top gear. *Weeks 41–44*: The distribution and exhibition deals are finalised and signed so that the showcasing space is confirmed. *Week 45*: The film is sent for local/international censoring and certification. *Week 48*: A major publicity event for the film is organised. *Weeks 49–50*: Satellite, online, and digital deals are closed so that content can be available for download/viewing as per the agreed schedule. As a rule of thumb, it is 100 days after the theatrical release of the movie. *Week 51*: The (secure and encrypted) film is dispatched across the world and loaded into servers for digital transmission. *Week 52*: All accounts associated with the film production are settled.	A marketing campaign requires the following components: – Launch tied-in merchandise with major retailers – Derive maximum mileage from the co-branding partner's marketing outlay and campaign – Specific target group marketing – Social media campaign activated from Week 2, with maximum traction is generated closer to the release date – Trailer is released globally on YouTube with an edited version broadcast as paid promotion on television – Posters and standee banners are dispatched to different locations – Print campaign commences, with advertisements and write-ups generated – Interviews with lead cast and crew are conducted and circulated in print and online media – The lead cast and crew undertake a promotional tour to major destinations to promote the movie through TV appearances, public space appearances, interviews and merchandise signing events.
Release and post-release	– The film is released to screens – Stocktake takes place to understand the reasons for the film's success or failure.	

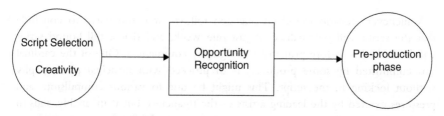

4.2 Pre-production

narration of the script (a process that lasts between three to six hours) and if the script is deemed to have potential then it moves to the next step of the process, including commissioning a team to create a full-bound script with dialogue and scene delineation.

When the full-bound script is ready after discussion, reviewing and editing, the script is approved, and the project is green-lit if it has commercial and artistic potential. Scriptwriting can be done by a specialist team of writers or in some instances the director also doubles up as a scriptwriter. If the story is poor or unappealing, then no amount of packaging in terms of a big-star cast and mind-blowing special effects can save the product. Ultimately, audiences want to be entertained, and they need a good story. It is crucial that the story is finalised, and all the wrinkles ironed out before principal photography commences. It is a recipe for disaster if the script is chopped and changed on-set while principal photography is taking place.

Scenario 2: An initiative from the director. The common turn of phrase employed in the movie industry to describe the scripting stage is 'development hell' (Kaire 2013). During this phase, the director is attempting to develop an interesting idea or subject into a viable screenplay that can be translated onto the screen. There is no guarantee the script will be approved and funded, thereby putting at risk months of development work. It is hellish because the director is trying to second-guess a producer and come up with material that they might appreciate. It is normal for the script to be pitched to several producers, and get passed around; getting a script approved by the first producer who sees it is rare. There are several instances where the one-line subject is approved but the project is dropped or shelved after the full script development fails to enthuse the producer

Scenario 3: An initiative from a leading artist. The leading artist can be a male lead, female lead or even a crucial supporting role. In this scenario, they find a script or story that has potential and—due to their inexperience in production, or lack of access to funds, or just plain risk-aversive nature—pitch it to a producer as a joint venture or a project in which the artist is willing to risk their remuneration by agreeing to a back-end deal. This scenario often enthuses the producer because of the artist's commitment to the project, thereby making it a little easier to pitch to potential buyers and distributors—depending on the marketability of the star.

Whichever scenario the script selection follows, it is too naive to conclude that the script will be finalised in just one week, and that a full-bound script will be locked in before principal photography commences. One of the cardinal sins committed by some producers is to proceed with principal photography without locking in the script. This might be due to various compulsions and pressures exerted by the leading artists or the financiers, but it invariably ends in disaster in terms of cost as well as eventual commercial failure.

In the case of Scenario 1 and Scenario 3, the producer narrows the field down to a suitable director who can visualise and interpret the script well. A leading producer comments on the experience of choosing a director as follows:

> I had major problems with directors A, B, C and D. The story was fantastic. Finally, when it was translated on to the screen, it was not good, I had clear cut no problem with director X, fantastic movies he did, in fact with me you know he gave only hits. You know why, if I give a script, when I green-light script, when he translates it will be a super hit. It will be better than the script, 200 per cent better, like I used to love him for that, what I thought is good humour he used to make it double the humour. I used to tell him, Boss you are a magician. Whereas when I see some script and I see it on screen, I feel my God what is this? This guy hasn't done anything. director Y I know very well will do it 100 per cent perfect, if I green-light a script, director Y will exactly deliver it. He will not under-deliver it, he will deliver exactly what is needed and I know that it will be a decent movie average to hit definitely not a flop.

Production

The production phase, as illustrated in Figure 4.3, entails team formation: a crucial part of the entrepreneurial process that can either facilitate or hinder movie success. Team formation includes the selection of cast and crew.

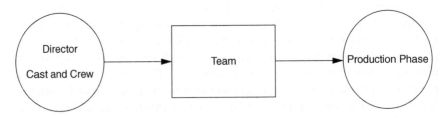

4.3   Team building and production

Identifying the appropriate director who can do justice to the script is a major challenge and a decision that will make or break the final outcome of the movie. Once that crucial decision is made, the production process commences. As mentioned earlier, the director is the captain and it is important that he or she is provided with a team that gives them reassurance rather than stress. Again, this is a critical component of any producer's remit: recruiting the right team really tests their skills in negotiating and making business decisions. Though every technician working for a movie is important, it is the main four that give maximum support to the director. They are: director of photography (DOP), the editor, music director and production designer. These four technicians help in transposing the director's vision onto the screen and presenting it in the way it was intended. It is not uncommon to hear and witness examples of the lead technicians walking out because of 'creative differences' with the director. The producer steps in to ensure that the working relationship is good between all the technicians. Even if a producer does not offer creative input, it is extremely crucial that the producer is adept at crisis management, so that tempers can be cooled and egos soothed.

Movie production can be compared to waging a war where there are several moving elements, all of which have to align in a strategic manner to win the battle. Those elements in movie production include: lauching the movie website and announcing the title; co-branding opportunities identified and finalised; the start of production planning; in-depth scheduling and planning are undertaken to work out the cost of production; delays and contingencies are factored in; and the budget is allotted into three categories—pre-production, production and post-production. Experienced producers are effective at calculating a tight budget allotment, adhering to the popular adage that 'movies don't fail, budgets do' (Johar 2016). Unrealistic budgets set up a project to fail; a seasoned and shrewd producer will lay out a realistic budget and always factor in project overruns and cost escalations. Once scheduling is complete, the logistics of implementing the schedule begin. As one leading producer, who has realised the importance of script through trial and error in his long career, commented:

> My sincere advice and I am of the opinion, especially in the cinema business, they should concentrate on the script first. Make the script ready, bound script, shot by shot we have to make it ready, then analyse when and where to shoot, count the number of days and also, in my opinion, the producer has to be physically present in the set. Everywhere, whether it is outdoor or indoor, unless that particular producer is physically present, it is very difficult to control online producers and other people because they are bound to go in an exorbitant manner, and we start losing in the project.

Over the years, moviemaking has evolved and what used to be a rule-of-thumb delineation of work has moved into professional demarcation, with 24 clearly identified departments in movie production. These 24 departments are also labelled as the 24 crafts of moviemaking (listed in Table 4.1). Many successful producers across the world have started their careers at the bottom, and they profess to the importance of understanding these crafts. It might not be possible to master all of the crafts, but a good producer will have a good grasp of them so that he or she can identify where bottlenecks can block progress, and create flow to prevent the project from being hindered. Film schools or formal education cannot substitute for the rich hands-on experience gained at the coalface of movie production. As a leading young producer, who began his journey early, as a fan of a particular star, and moved into production, remarked:

> After a period, at a point I thought that let us start production. So, I went to a top producer and I was working there so that I can learn the ropes of production for five to six months. I was with him and I was taking care as an assistant assisting the production manager, just observing things and trying to learn. That was initial schooling in production, and I learnt a lot there.

Along with the producer, as captain of the project, the director will be involved in the process of reruiting and hiring all the other technicians. During the same time period, suitable lead and supporting artists will be identified and the script will be sent to those artists. If Option A does not work out for a certain role, then there should be backup Options B and C. Some artists might suggest corrections or modifications to the script based on their interpretation of the role and their ability to enact that role. Detailed discussion and analysis are completed for each role with the director and the scriptwriters taking input from the artists and fine-tuning according to the requirements of the artist and the role.

Post-production

The post-production phase, illustrated in Figure 4.4, entails film-making and marketing—more key elements of the entrepreneurial process that can facilitate

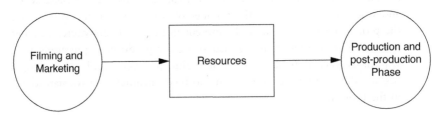

4.4 Post-production and release

or hinder the success of a movie. Film-making and marketing are part of the resource-allocation process in the entrepreneurial process.

Once principal photography or shooting concludes, the first marketing collateral—normally a first glimpse of the production or a digital motion poster —is released. With this, movie marketing officially commences. Post-production activities like editing, dubbing, sound mixing and colour grading are completed. During this period, producers exhibit a promotional reel or parts of the movie to various sections of the audience for test-marketing purposes. Generally, this audience tends to be drawn from the wider movie fraternity, such as distributors, exhibitors, movie school students or the peer groups of creative personnel. Their feedback is incorporated on the editing table and, if feasible, necessary modifications are made. In extreme cases, there might be a reshoot of a small portion or a 'patchwork shoot' to fill gaps or enhance the quality of the visual content. The movie release date is officially announced, and the marketing activities kick into top gear. Though there are budget constraints, every movie has to undertake a 360-degree marketing campaign.

A senior producer who began his journey as a distributor, designing his own publicity, and moved up to become a top producer, explains his unique marketing philosophyl; one that helped him survive for 50 years in the industry:

> I was designing the poster and publicity material. For me, the movie poster was very important. In my area the posters used to be pasted on Thursday or Friday, the poster used to be so attractive, and it would cause a traffic jam. The poster I designed and stuck used to be so popular that they used to wait for the poster design from me and fans used to wait for it and onlookers used to stop and stare at it causing a traffic jam. I used to flood the town with posters. My posters used to be new; they used to convey a dialogue or a story. The poster itself used to convey a story, there might not be a relevant connection between the scene, poster and the movie, but curiosity used to be aroused.

Once the marketing campaign kicks into top gear, the distribution and exhibition deals are finalised and signed so that the showcasing space is confirmed. This will ensure the major chains, as well as independent cinema theatres, schedule the movie for their screens. It is easier to *make* a movie than to *release* a movie. While the movie is being shot, the producer's money is being spent, so it is simpler than the release phase when other people's money and commitment is involved. A good producer always keeps an eye out for the marketing and distribution of the movie; this is the opportunity to showcase his or her strengths. While shooting, it is the director who calls the shots, but after shooting the ability of a producer to get maximum attention comes into play. The movie content is sent to different parts of the world for censoring and certification. Normally, the turnaround time for this process is two to four weeks, so the process needs to be completed within this time. Exhibitors will not begin booking unless the movie is censored and certified.

Four weeks before the release, a major event is organised, such as launching the soundtrack or a glitzy star-studded premiere that receives wide publicity and generous media coverage. In order for the movie to be available for download and viewing as per the agreed schedule, the satellite, online and digital deals need to be closed. As a rule of thumb, this is generally 100 days after the theatrical release of the movie. Just a few days prior to this, the content of the movie will be dispatched to different screens across the world and loaded onto servers for digital transmission. It is double-checked to ensure that the encryption and security codes are in place so that security of the content is not compromised. All accounts need to be settled. Any dues to the artists, technicians, equipment suppliers and studio lots should be paid, and a no-dues letter should be collected. Money from the buyers and distributors needs to be collected if the movie is sold on an outright basis. The security code must be issued to all the screens across the world with clear parameters set for the screening time.

The movie finally hits the screens … its fate will be decided by lunchtime. Reviews will be out and the producers, director and cast will know the outcome by the number of phone calls they receive! If the movie is declared a disaster, the marketing campaign ends immediately as a way of cutting losses. If the movie is declared an average gross, the marketing spend is increased and ensures that the campaign fires on all cylinders for at least three weeks after release. This guarantees that exhibitors continue screening the movie and thereby increases potential revenue. If the movie is declared a super hit, word of mouth will carry the movie and the marketing campaign can be sustained for two more weeks. There is generally no need to enhance the spend because everyone will be marketing the successful movie.

Following the movie's release, the time to take stock arrives. This is done with a thorough post-mortem to understand the reasons for the movie's success or failure. If it is a success, the potential exists to sell the rights of the story in different languages or to take the movie onto the festival circuit to generate additional revenue. And, of course, there will be a big party to celebreate the success. The media can't get enough of a success story, but they often remain choosy.

If the movie is a failure, ways to minimise losses can be sought through selling at bargain rates to pay-per-view TV, or dubbing it into different languages to increase revenue and recover some of the losses. In this case, the press will avoid the team and, to be in circulation, the team either announces the next big project or retreats quietly from view.

In a similar way to normal life—but exaggerated in showbusiness where fortunes change every Friday—success has many parents, yet failure is an orphan. Though the producer is not listed in the 24 crafts of movie production, the irreplaceable and entrepreneurial role of a producer is highlighted at every stage of the project. The producer is deeply involved and keeps the project moving forward as someone who connects all of the moving parts. An interesting insight is that every one of those 24 craftspeople is paid by the producer—this one insight provides sufficient evidence to establish the supremacy of the producer, who is not one among them, but above them.

Conclusion

The process of green-lighting and resourcing a project entails the most crucial decisions that a producer must make. The production house with which Rajeev was involved read close to 100 scripts for the 14 movies that eventually made it onto the screen. In the movie production business, producers are bombarded with scripts on an almost daily basis. Despite the critical nature of these decisions and the potential impact they have on the financial well-being of a producer and production house, the green-lighting decision is made in an ad hoc manner, as explained, relying on judgement and intuition that cannot be submitted to analytical reasoning. This results in green-lighting being influenced from various quarters and thereby delivering unpredictable results. It is imperative that producers expend more energy on this crucial aspect of moviemaking, and even movie schools should inculcate some basic guiding principles for green-lighting projects.

From experience, it can be concluded that what cannot be fixed at the script stage cannot be fixed at the shooting stage for the simple reason that the fault becomes magnified. It is surprising that such a crucial decision in this entrepreneurial process is treated in a lackadaisical manner. Business potential guiding the selection of scripts is a healthy trend, and at least serves as a warning signal for producers who tend to risk too much or let their gambling instincts take over the practical side of making business decisions. However, problems do crop up when, instead of heeding logical business potential, producers start green-lighting projects based on imagined and assumed potential, such as a director's or star's past record of success. These factors may ensure that the project receives good press and hype, resulting in good opening-weekend numbers, but the ensuing damage will be too high, with loss of credibility and reputation for the producer. This places enormous pressure on the next green-lighting decision. In conclusion, as long as green-lighting decisions are made based on cold logic and hard business figures, the chances of failure decrease and any other factors that creep into consideration for this crucial decision will imperil success.

References

Johar, K 2016, 'Movies don't fail, budgets do', *Mid-Day.com*, 4 October, accessed 28/10/18, www.mid-day.com/articles/karan-johar-movies-dont-fail-budgets-do/17655185.

Kaire, S, 2013, 'Development Hell', *Script*, 4 October, accessed 27/01/18, www.scriptmag.com/features/development-hell.

Timmons, JA, Muzyka, DF, Stevenson, HH and Bygrave, WD 1987, 'Opportunity recognition: The core of entrepreneurship', in N C Churchill et al. (ed), *Frontiers of Entrepreneurship Research*, pp. 109–123, Babson College, Wellesley, MA.

PART III

Entrepreneurial Indian movie producers

5

MANAGING INDIAN MOVIE STARS
Starry tantrums, combination craze

If two men on a job agree all the time, then one is useless. If they disagree all the time, then both are useless.

Darryl F Zanuck, legendary Hollywood producer

Introduction

The movie business relies on the suspension of belief and audience reaction to the narrative on screen. When a patron buys a ticket for cinema, he or she might have several motivating factors. They might crave entertainment, or wish to relax after a long day's work, or they might want intellectual stimulation, or even critical analysis. The challenge for a movie producer is to ensure all these factors are represented in the movie so that the whole audience finds it worthy of their time and money. This challenge becomes daunting when the producer has the unenviable task of managing a cast and crew numbering in the hundreds for a major motion picture. How stars and directors behave is an additional entrepreneurial risk that can jeopardise the venture. In the 21st century, despicable behaviour in the movie industry is being called out through the global #MeToo campaign. India is no different. This chapter examines some of the starry tantrums and 'combination crazes'—searching for the right combination that works at the box office —that producers need to manage for the movie venture to succeed.

Cinema is the epitome of teamwork, and it is unheard of for one person to perform all the roles that are essential for making a movie. If one member of the team behaves badly, the end result will suffer. Furthermore, some adventurous people have tried to make a movie by themselves, undertaking all the tasks. The results are not worth mentioning. It is almost impossible to create a quality movie without the effort of an entire team. But a team that is brimming with talent and creativity is fertile terrain for conflicts, ego clashes and starry tantrums. Every technician that works on a movie is a creative artist: the composer, the director of photography, the editor and the director, who manages the entire process according to their vision and guides the team towards that end.

This vision of the end product is the source of many conflicts in the movie industry, as each member of the team has a different angle on that vision. Stories of creative egos getting bruised on the sets of every—yes every—movie production are common. Imagine a scene from the 2018 release, *The Post*, a gripping movie with a fair share of creative artists on board. When the audience sees Meryl Streep and Tom Hanks on screen in a dramatic scene, they are seeing the work of artists who have won 17 Academy Awards between them. Meryl Streep has won three, Tom Hanks has won two, the director Steven Spielberg has won two, composer John Williams has won five, the editor Michael Kahn has won three and the director of photography Janusz Kaminski, two. This is an incredible number. The movie therefore showcases talent of the highest calibre. Needless to say, the audience gave their stamp of approval through the box office returns of US$180 million against a budget of US$50 million. It is inevitable that such talent will create friction, but this example highlights the fact that Spielberg has worked with the same crew for several movies and, incredibly, with the same composer for his entire career. This exemplifies that, as a 'captain', Spielberg is comfortable with his team and remains true to them irrespective of the box office outcome. Many other directors have not been as successful in gluing together such a team, and stories of tantrums and walkouts abound, involving technicians as well as the leading artists.

Starry tantrums

Indian cinema operates largely within the confines of the star system, something akin to Hollywood in the late 1940s and 1950s. However, the stars in Indian cinema, in the majority of cases, become trapped inside a commercial image created for them. They main reason they fail to emerge from this image is due to fear of rejection by the audience. The two following examples illustrate this point:

> Example 1: It is universally accepted that the shelf life of leading men is much longer than leading ladies, but in the case of Indian cinema, it was stretched to a new dimension. As discussed in Chapter 2, South Indian cinema was dominated by stars like MGR and NTR, who were very image-conscious and used to go to ridiculous lengths to protect their image. Leading ladies paired to play opposite them became younger and younger as the years passed. In fact, girls who previously acted as daughters or granddaughters started playing heroines. This meant that 60-year-old male leads were dancing and romancing girls as young as 16 to 18 years, reportedly catering to the audience's desire that their heroes never age. Having teenage heroines helped perpetuate this myth.

Example 2: Audiences may accept or reject experimentation with a star's image. The commercial confines of Indian cinema can be more limiting in this respect than has been the case in Hollywood. In 1990 the movie *Agnee-path* (*Path of Fire*) was released, starring one of the biggest superstars, Amitabh Bachchan. The movie is a routine revenge/vendetta drama, but failed at the box office. The main reason attributed to its failure was that Bachchan experimented with his voice. Part of the image of an Indian movie star is their voice, which is part and parcel of their image—more so in the case of Bachchan, who has a deep baritone. When he tried to experiment with his voice, in a similar way to Marlon Brando in *The Godfather*, the audience rejected it. The producer had to re-issue movie prints in its second week with advertisements highlighting the movie now had the 'original voice' by Bachchan. Here we see the difference in the power of an image between the two industries. The audience loved Brando's rendition of Don Corleone in *The Godfather*, and he was rewarded with box office glory as well as an Academy Award. Bachchan, however, was pilloried for messing with his voice and faced rejection and box office failure, forcing him to re-dub his role for the movie. The audience of *The Godfather* welcomed experimentation with open arms, whereas the audience of *Agneepath* rejected it.

Fear of rejection forces Indian movie stars to stay inside the comfort zone of their image. This trend was predominant from the 1970s to the 1990s, yet, with the advent of the new millennium, the audience started to change and today there is more acceptance and flexibility when it comes to the image of a star. In fact, audience and fans alike expect their heroes to experiment a little and therefore set trends rather than follow them. Experimenting with image tends to be a point of friction between producer and star. This is due to the producer's need to ensure a commercially viable venture rather than to cater to the whims of the star. However, for the star, the producer is viewed as a means for furthering and enhancing their image and someone who must not do anything that results in conflict. Otherwise, tantrums follow, and they are definitely one of the more stressful aspects of movie production:

> A leading star had seven consecutive box office disasters. The production company made a conscious decision to showcase the male and female leads, as well as the prominent supporting cast, in all publicity material. This was done to reduce the risk of exposure to the negative image currently surrounding the male lead after consecutive box office debacles. Though promotion and marketing are the prerogatives of the producer, leading artists are involved so that they commit to including promotions in their schedule, thereby enhancing the visibility of the forthcoming release. In this case, the male lead was annoyed. He threw a major tantrum, refusing to dub his portions of the movie because he believed the producer was side-stepping him to deliberately harm his career.

No amount of reasoning from the producer worked. The producer refused to relent, threatening to get the dubbing completed by a voice-over artist. Sensing the damage this stalemate was doing to the forthcoming release, on which his future rested, the actor relented and obtained assurances from the producer that all future publicity will place him in prominence. Luckily, this movie succeeded at the box office. Both the producer and star moved on without bad blood. This shows how all the effort and money invested in a project by a producer can be held at ransom by the tantrum of a star.

Such tantrums *before* a project commences are in some ways less damaging because the producer can be assertive and decide to call off the project with minimal financial loss. As one senior producer with 38 years' experience—and who made the bold decision to call off a project due to starry tantrums—explained, stars can be very self-centred, with a bad attitude and an unprofessional manner. For example: 'The star had a bad attitude. He was very unprofessional. I did not like his attitude. In the industry we see many people with such a mentality because they are very self-centred, and they do not think of others.'

The same producer recounted his experience of replacing three directors to cater to the ego-driven demands of the star:

> There are still some individuals in this industry who have the moral fabric and ethical conviction to stick to their standpoint, but sadly this is a very rare species today.
>
> The movie was green-lit and after that the star asked the director to direct the movie for his own company. [...] The star calls me and says that he wants to change the director and he wanted me to get another award-winning director. This veteran director is a great man, may his soul rest in peace. He returned all the money that I gave him as an advance and though I spent money on the planning and pre-production, he understood my position and returned his advance. [...] Then I went back to the star and told him that I didn't want to do a project with the award-winning director and I would drop the project. I had given the star an advance amount, but he returned only 50 per cent of it. Until today he has not returned the balance amount.

Tantrums are not the exclusive domain of the stars. Directors have been known to walk off sets and order everyone to pack up the day's shooting if they are unhappy. The financial impact of such tantrums is ultimately borne by the producer because losing one day's shooting means losing all the expenses for that day because everyone has to be paid irrespective of whether any shots were successfully completed or not. There is a high chance of friction between the producer and the director if their creative visions do not match and both take a rigid stance, ultimately damaging the project irrespective of who is proven right.

The friction between John Ford and Darry F Zanuck, and arguments between William Wyler and Sam Goldwyn are part of Hollywood folklore now. All these individuals had strong vision and conviction and were reluctant to budge from their viewpoints. It can be argued, though, that the friction helped create masterpieces like *The Grapes of Wrath* or *The Best Years of our Lives.*

One strong-minded mid-career producer, who had his share of run-ins with his directors, recounts the time he had a protest and sit-in from his director and the creative team due to major differences in the artistic and commercial perception of the movie:

> We had a major fight, major fight. The movie was a washout at the box office. My prediction came true. I lost my entire investment plus interest and publicity costs in the movie. As producer I was very clear that this is not the ending that we want, this is an artistic climax, and we wanted a commercial climax.

The crux of the matter was the producer arguing that the audience does not want the protagonist to be killed.

> You are killing the protagonist—when the protagonist is killed the movie is killed. As a producer, I will lose all the money. So, if you like it so much then you take the risk and buy the movie and release it yourself. The director and the supporting star said NO they do not have the money therefore they cannot be responsible.

However, their differences were not resolved:

> One month later I got a warning message that they are going to go on a protest march and fast unto death saying that this guy is not releasing the movie. Then I called my board and informed them about this latest threat, ok I don't know what to do. This is not me as an individual, I can face it and fight it, but the production house brand name should not suffer. So, the Chair convened a board meeting and asked me how much we will lose, I said we will lose our entire investment. They said the company name is bigger because it is one of the world's leading names in entertainment, and they will not like their name to be dragged into this controversy. They said let's bite the bullet, let us release the movie and face the losses. Ok whatever it is let us face it, now you put it on record that this loss is expected.

The producer informed the director that he is 'releasing the movie under coercion and force' but with a 'phenomenal marketing campaign' so that no one can blame him:

But my judgement is not wrong, commercially if I cannot judge the outcome of my own product then I should not be in the industry. We did a phenomenal campaign; we released the movie and the movie tanked within one day. So what I am saying is that as a producer, are you prepared sufficiently to handle the failure financially as well as reputation wise. I was prepared, I prepared my ground for failure.

In these three examples of starry tantrums, the producer faces the brunt of the damage. Losses of money, reputation and the breakdown of the relationship haunt any producer who gets embroiled in such tantrums. Therefore, it is the producer who tends to compromise and yield to the pressure. It is the producer who stands to gain the most financially if the movie succeeds. Therefore, the producer is always on the lookout for the right combination to increase the chances of success. This combination can be the leading male and female artists, like Bogart and Bacall, or a leading director and leading artist like Almodovar and Cruz, or Chopra and Shahrukh Khan. Combinations like these assure producers of attention in business circles, and curiosity from the audience: both increase the chances of commercial viability. For a producer who wants to defeat the odds of failure, it is natural to pursue this combination craze.

Combination craze

A producer once remarked that he always used to make movies that kept everyone happy, including the distributors, the exhibitors, concession/candy-bar team and even the parking lot attendants. Although loaded with hyperbole, the remark highlights the bottom line that the livelihoods and survival of several players depends on the success of the movie. It is natural for everyone to chase the right combination of factors, especially if that combination has delivered success before, because there is a greater chance that it will again. In a way, the craze for combination is an insurance policy that ensures order in the chaotic world of movies. There are producers who excel in stitching together the right combination, being one that yields rich box office dividends. As noted in Chapter 2, in the Malayalam movie industry of yesteryear, the star Prem Nazir was paired with Sheela in 130 movies. Apart from being a record-breaking feat, this points to the fact that producers, directors and the audience all drew comfort from the well-known pairing and set their expectationss according to the familiar combination. This craze for successful combinations is reflected in how a particular director becomes comfortable with a set of technicians and is reluctant to alter the synchronicity of their collective creativity. This is why someone like Spielberg works with the same crew. A senior producer who maintained the same cast and crew for three consecutive projects recounts:

I did a movie, it did reasonably well. It was a successful combo of my earlier movie, and the same combination of that movie was being repeated, so I knew I can pre-sell the movie, I knew if I can control the production budget then I will be able to recover. So that was more of a calculated decision you make and produce, it is more like a project assembling knowing very well the potential for the project and its outcome. Financially it worked out well for me, career-wise it was ok, not as big as the previous one nothing too good, but it was ok. Nothing to take out but ok.

However, the craze for stitching together the right combinations can end in disaster if the budget is not adhered to. Many producers make the wrong assumption that the market will expand, and take the risk of increasing the cost of production. Though it is a fact that the market does occasionally increase for a successful combination, this must be treated with caution. The expansion of the market might not match the gamble that a producer is willing to take. As one young producer who graduated from the ranks of line production and executive production remarked:

> A new, young, leading actor received a paltry sum of $10,000 as his remuneration because it was just his second movie and even the audience had not accepted him completely. Luckily this movie was released, and it was declared a blockbuster.

The success of the movie caused the actor to become over-confident in his ability and success after becoming 'the hottest new talent in the market'.

> Producers started making a beeline for this actor. After that movie, I was supposed to produce a movie with this actor, and I was thinking of offering him $40,000 which is four times more than the remuneration for his earlier, but another new producer came in and offered him $400,000 straight away. Needless to say, this blind combination craze backfired and the movie lost its entire investment and the producer was bankrupt with crippling debts that forced him out of the industry. I am telling this because this is a bad habit that many producers follow, in their quest for the hottest combination in the market, they do not hesitate to offer mouth-watering deals to the stars only to realise that the business potential is non-existent. That desperation is the killer that ruins business in this industry. On the other side I have worked with a producer who never gets swayed by this combination craze and sticks to his budget and succeeds.

Combination craze stems from the early days in Hollywood when producers were always on the lookout for a bankable cast to bankroll their productions, thereby locking stars into annual contracts. Once the stars were locked into contracts with the studios, producers used to shop around for material suitable for their contract actors. They looked for material from the theatres of Broadway or the West End or popular literary works from across the continents. This template was also followed in the Indian movie industry. In the early 1970s, however, the contract system collapsed as studios lost influence and independent producers gained momentum in combination with star-power asserting itself. The majority of producers opt for the safer option of cashing in on a trend rather than the riskier option of setting the trend. Many enterprising producers have learnt the hard way that movies that are way ahead of their time often fail to connect with the audience and, at the end of the day, whether at nickelodeons, tent cinemas or multi-screen complexes, the ticket-buying public expect entertainment, not education. Movie producers are entrepreneurs in the true sense when they cash in on an opportunity, and a successful combination that previously worked at the box office is an opportunity worth pursuing.

Conclusion

This chapter began with a quote from Darryl F Zanuck, one of the greatest Hollywood movie producers, that captures the nature of tantrums as well as combinations in a nutshell. Moviemaking is a team effort—a creative team effort —unlike a factory production operation, which, while relying on team effort, is short on creativity. There are bound to be debates, discussions and friction in this creative process and, if the greater good of the project is kept in mind and everyone works towards the same goal, the outcome will be positive. However, if individual egos come into play and pull the project in different directions, the end result can be disastrous. When stars are throwing tantrums or when the combination touted to work so well comes unstuck, the one person who has to keep cool and manage the entire process is the producer.

This chapter dealt with two of the most compelling issues that a producer confronts. From personal experience, a producer has every right to halt or call off the project as this is a crucial decision faced by every entrepreneur. A project that is not going according to plan has to be called off, particularly if there is no hope of it improving. Otherwise it will become a classic example of throwing good money after bad. No matter what the cast and crew think, or whatever the financial and reputational implications are, a producer has to show courage when calling off a project. If it is not called off, then finances and reputations will take a major hit when the movie is deemed to be a disaster. A portion of the financial disaster can be averted if the producer cancels the project. An entrepreneurial producer is one who has control over all the aspects of the project regardless of stars or crew. The final authority must always rest with the producer. If control is relinquished, no crazy combination can prevent the slide from hopeful blockbuster to disaster.

6

BLOCKBUSTERS AND BOMBS IN THE INDIAN MOVIE BUSINESS

Success ruins more people in this business than failure.

Samuel Goldwyn

Introduction

The poignant quote about success and failure by one of Hollywood's original moguls, renowned for 'the Goldwyn touch' in moviemaking, points out the quintessential yardstick of success and failure in the movie industry. A star, a director and a producer are only as good as their last success. Hollywood legends like Thalberg, Goldwyn, Zanuck, Mayer and Warner (Jack) had their fair share of failures but their ability to bounce back and come up with the next venture to erase the memory of failure bestowed legendary status on them.

In the Indian movie industry, the only surviving studio or production house that is into the fourth generation of owners is AVM. Every other studio and production house ceased operations by the third generation. RK studios, established by the legendary Raj Kapoor stopped production years ago, in 1999. Raj Kapoor was a titan among producers in Indian cinema: an early pioneer who placed Indian cinema on the world map and had a genuine fan following in the Soviet Union and Japan. Unfortunately, his successors were unable to keep the production house running, despite all of them having worked in the movie industry with various degrees of success. Yash Raj Movies is being managed by its second generation and is a prolific production house with business interest spanning production and distribution. Dharma Productions is also being managed by the second generation and has significant output on its own and in collaboration with other production houses. Third and fourth generations of the Barjatya family have taken control of Rajshri productions and have expanded the footprint from just movies into the digital space, books and television; it has reinvented itself as a complete media and entertainment company. Unfortunately, these few are the only examples of Indian movie studios and production houses that have survived into the 21st century. Unlike Hollywood, where Warner, Disney, Universal, MGM and Paramount have survived more than, or close to, 100 years, in Indian cinema only AVM and Rajshri have survived for more than 70 years.

Longevity need not be a measure of success. But in the eyes of the general public, a brand that survives for four generations will enjoy a higher degree of goodwill and carry a positive image, as it must be doing something right to last so many years. In this case, the difference between Hollywood and Indian cinema lies in the family-controlled operations as opposed to professional management. Every Hollywood studio mentioned above is a publicly listed company with shareholders, a professional board and a management team to run operations. Every Indian movie studio and production house mentioned so far is family-owned and operated, closely scrutinised and controlled by members of the founding family. This might be one of the reasons why companies don't last beyond the third generation. As generations change, their preferences and choices may change, adding to the uncertainty. Nostalgia aside, a studio or production house can only be in business as long as it is commercially viable. Rajeev has witnessed several studios being converted into residential apartments, shopping complexes and hotels. The land on which these studios were located is commercially attractive, so it does not make business sense to run them as loss-making studios with all the associated debilitating overhead costs attached. It is important to note that none of the studios closed down when they were making money but were forced to close down once they began accumulating losses. In the movie industry, success and failure inevitably go hand in hand and they tend to follow each other as day follows night. A successful producer overcomes financial losses from their failures by means of the revenues from success. In the long run, if a producer's blockbusters far outnumber their disasters, there is a greater chance for their production house staying in business for longer.

Blockbusters

During the Second World War, large bombs capable of destroying blocks of houses or buildings were dropped for the first time. These were called 'blockbuster' bombs. Gradually, this word entered the cinema vernacular, especially to describe very successful movies. In the days of single screens, before multi-screen complexes were conceived, people had to line up at the ticket counter to purchase tickets. Movies like *Gone with the Wind, Jaws* and *Star Wars* witnessed unprecedented crowds and the queues for ticket sales extended for several blocks. Such cultural phenomena and trend-setting movies were became known as blockbusters. Indian cinema had its fair share of blockbusters, and though it might seem unbelievable, there was a movie that ran for 23 consecutive years on one screen in Mumbai, eclipsing the previous record of five years.

On 15th August 1975, exactly 28 years after India attained independence from British rule, a movie was released. This movie redefined the boundaries of Indian box office and continues to enthral movie students and aficionados even 44 years later. That movie, *Sholay* (*Embers*), produced by GP Sippy and directed by his son Ramesh Sippy, was an Indian adaptation of Sergio Leone's spaghetti western movies. It is a guns-for-hire saga of two small-time criminals hired by a former cop to avenge a crime committed upon him and his family by a dreaded dacoit. It was the second 70 mm movie released in India and went on to become the movie with the largest box office gross of all time. Reams of literature have been written to analyse *Sholay's* unprecedented success, and doctoral theses research the *Sholay* phenomenon. However, to put it simply, *Sholay's* success lies in entertainment. It was and is a very entertaining movie with foot-tapping music, rib-tickling comedy, spine-chilling villainy, tears, joy and the ultimate triumph of good over evil but at a price. All of this, packaged into three hours in a large-screen format, ensured that Indian audiences lapped it up. A single-screen theatre, the Minerva, known as the pride of Maharashtra (the Indian state in which it was situated) screened *Sholay* continuously for five years, three of which screened the regular three shows per day; for the following two years, it was screened as a matinee. For almost one year, tickets had to be booked well in advance and the demand kept growing and spread across the country. The British Film Institute ranks *Sholay* in its top ten movies of all time. In addition to the unprecedented box office returns, *Sholay* also pushed the boundaries for technical excellence in Indian cinema. At that time, it was doubtful any other movie could break *Sholay's* record of a continuous run of 286 weeks in a single screen; however, 20 years later the record was threatened and then broken.

Dilwale Dulhania Le Jayenge (*DDLJ*) (in English, *The Large-Hearted Will Take the Bride*) could almost be called the polar opposite of *Sholay*. With its saccharine theme of romance and family values, *DDLJ* captured the imagination of the new India that was experiencing the freedom and liberation unleashed by economic reform in 1991.Also, the younger generation identified with the male and female leads. The brain drain that symbolised India's years of socialist politics created a sense of nostalgia for the homeland by non-resident Indians who yearned to come back to their roots. These themes were central in *DDLJ*. The music was another major factor as the songs of *DDLJ* became the anthems for young India and helped catapult *Sholay* to the top of the box office charts. It was natural at this time for *DDLJ's* romantic young male lead to break the record of *Sholay's* angry young man. Maratha Mandir, a single screen in Mumbai, presented *DDLJ* continuously for 23 years—more than 1,200 weeks.

Nowadays, with the demise of single screens, it can be safely predicted that this record will not be eclipsed in the near future and perhaps never. In the past, movies could play for up to one year if they were popular. However, the long run for movies has lost its relevance. Long-running movies do not earn any more money. The number of screens has increased significantly, allowing movies to be played in multiplexes. In many cases, the revenue from the entire run of a movie in the 1970s is now collected during the first weekend of a contemporary release. This is due to the increase in screens, the saturation of screens running a movie, and the advent of digital technology that makes it easier to release moves on as many screens as possible. The old analogue technology was restricted by the number of prints released and the number of screens. The process of screening from a print was cumbersome as the print had to be physically rewound and reloaded and the chances of damaging the print were very high. Projectionists had to be ever-vigilant to prevent the print from getting cut up or burnt. Such physical challenges restricted the number of screens that could exhibit. To reduce the cost of multiple prints, one print would be shared between two or three screens, and transported between multiple locations. Producers used to cherish a long run of their movies and held celebrations to mark successful runs of 100 days, a 25 week silver jubilee and 50 weeks golden jubilee. Theatre owners were invited to these celebrations and presented with shields or mementoes to commemorate success. Theatres displayed these shields in the lobby and display cabinets became a matter of pride for the owners and movie fans.

Producers enjoy top bragging rights when it comes to describing the success of a blockbuster. Rajeev recounts his personal experience, following a stressful week before the release of a movie, walking down the aisle of a cinema as the audience applauded a sequence, prompting tears to stream down his cheeks. This is one of the best moments in any movie producer's journey.

Here, a very successful producer and director recounts his experiences with two blockbusters. His first blockbuster told the story of the making of a fantasy movie where the star dies, goes to hell and brings about a revolution in hell. It was a comedy featuring a parody of Yama, the God of Death, aka Lucifer. A famous director with many successful movies to his name, he explains how the producer was baited by a star who set an unrealistic twenty-seven-day timeframe for the movie's completion. The bait was set to try and get the star out of having to act in the movie. Surprisingly, the producer took the bait:

> My biggest blockbuster came about like this. The producer was in financial trouble. He was from the same village as the star. He requested help to get out of the financial mess he was in. At that point the leading actor said that he had 27 day-call sheets available that were allotted to another producer for a project that would probably not get

off the ground—so he said those dates are available. This desperate producer said yes immediately and committed to the project. He did not think about the budget or remuneration or any other costings, he just said yes because it was a lifeline for him. Then he comes rushing into our office and tells us the star has agreed to do the movie and we have 27 days from him to complete it.

The director's emotion is illustrated in his outburst to the producer:

> I was wild and yelled at him, asking whether I was directing the movie or whether he was! How the hell can he agree for 27 days? How can I complete a movie in 27 days? Then the producer explained to me, saying: 'Let us get into it first and, after the midway point, ask the hero for extra days, he won't disagree. Let's start. There is no better opportunity than this and we will have to complete it come what may'. Since all of us were technicians, we had that borderline arrogant certainty that we could pull it off even though it was a complex subject with massive sets, a huge budget and the risky concept of the God of Death coming down to earth. Somehow we were still confident.

The result of this gambit was astonishing: the movie was completed in 27 days and became a blockbuster:

> We got into it and worked like crazy to ensure that the entire movie was completed in 27 days. Yes, the entire shoot was completed in 27 days: everything, including the songs and fights, were completed in 27 days. Whatever the cause or whatever the problems we faced during shooting the movie became a blockbuster.

The same director tried to replicate this success with another producer. The second movie was a tragedy in contrast to the first movie. It worked because of the pathos of the subject matter:

> This movie was a super hit, I shot a song with a dead body and the song is immortal now. After release, I watched the movie in a matinee since I was shooting close by. I went to the single-screen theatre and watched it with the audience. There was thunderous applause in the auditorium and the audience response was superb. For a moment, I was not sure if the audience was praising the film or being sarcastic. The lyric was appreciated so much, and it talks about sharing the burden and repaying parents. The hero comes running and lends a hand in carrying a body, while not knowing that it is his mother's body. That song was historic, and the movie was a blockbuster. Even

today after many years and almost 100 movies as a producer and director, everyone remembers me as the creator of these two blockbusters.

From these examples, blockbuster success is seen to be a mix of recognising the correct opportunity, taking a calculated risk, executing it within budget and marketing so that it has a wide reach. However, there is an element of chance —like when a movie made in 27 days becomes a blockbuster—that is unique to the movie industry and is not explained in detail in the existing literature on entrepreneurship.

The producer of the first blockbuster described above could not mount any further projects and eventually stopped production. However, the producer of the second blockbuster is still active and the production house is managed by the second and third generation with fewer productions but more joint ventures and distribution work. Night has to follow day and disasters tend to follow blockbusters. The makers of both *Sholay* and *DDLJ* had their fair share of disasters but the production house that made *DDLJ*, Yash Raj Movies is one of the leading such houses in India. At the time of writing, the producer of *Sholay* has not produced a movie in the past six years.

In the next section, we discuss Indian movies which bombed at the box office and the reasons why they were failures for the entrepreneurs involved.

Bombs

It is ironic that a bomb can be used as a metaphor for both success and failure in the movie industry. Just like a big success is described as a blockbuster, a failure is described as the movie having bombed or flopped. It is difficult to pinpoint the exact the reason for failure but it is safe to assume that a movie fails because of an unrealistic budget. If the budget of a movie is far higher than the market potential, then the chances of financial disaster are significantly higher. Many movie producers commit the fundamental error of gambling on success due to an inflated budget. In their hearts, they know that the potential for the movie is only n dollars, but they spend much more than that hoping that it will be a blockbuster or a sleeper hit and miraculously recover much more than predicted. As in real life, miracles are rare in the movie business. This contributes to a very high rate of failure in the industry. It is interesting to hear about the vicious trap of failure from a financier who had a ringside view of movie production. This example illustrates that irrational risk-taking is a type of gambling:

> Why does the industry still exist, despite such a high rate of failure? That is a question we have always asked. When we look at the hard numbers, in my view even a 90 per cent failure rate is an optimistic number because a lot of producers don't want to openly state the financial outcome of a movie because they always project it as a positive. There are two reasons for this.

First is the image of a successful producer, who wants to keep his failures to himself and who doesn't want to broadcast them outside. Second, his ability to borrow further sums from various lenders is drastically affected if the lenders know that he has failed before and is sitting on huge loans.

There are the regular gamblers, the guys who raise money from others, who are constantly in debt and who always say they have some movie under production and tell the lenders, 'Listen I have this movie, when the movie releases, I will collect and pay you back'. These are the guys who are trying for the next blockbuster with somebody else's money. There are a bunch of producers who are running around. If you look at the professional production houses that have come to India from Hollywood, or some of the home-grown production houses, even those people bat for a few years and come out with some successes and some failures. After some time they also pack up and enter other streams within the industry which are more predictable. Streams like distribution for a commission business or getting into the theatre-screening business, or the equipment business, or any of those kinds of businesses.

A majority of new producers face this challenge and end up with financial disasters on their hands. One producer succinctly commented that: 'movie production is risk management. If we jump from the first floor, the chances of surviving with a few broken bones are high, but if we jump from the tenth floor, the chances of surviving are remote.'

Producers who take calculated risks are jumping from the first floor but producers who gamble are jumping from the tenth. Some producers are diligent in controlling costs and do not exceed the rigid restrictions placed on their budgetary limits. Such producers have less exposure to bombs. Barring unforeseen natural calamities, careful planning, control of the budget and proper release showcasing ensures that the chances of disaster are reduced. But how many producers do adhere to these conventions is a moot question. While successfully exploiting entrepreneurial opportunities is the primary aim of all entrepreneurship initiatives (Shepherd and Patzelt 2017) entrepreneurial success and failure can be unpredictable. But by bootstrapping, controlling the budget and reducing the risk of financial exposure, the chances of success are higher.

Conclusion

An entrepreneur has to prepare for success and failure, but there is a significant gap between blockbuster success and disastrous failure. This significant gap represents the difference between continuing or ceasing as an entrepreneur. Some entrepreneurs who continue after a failure manage a turnaround in their fortunes by developing skills and competencies through the experience of failure—in other words, through entrepreneurial learning (Sardana and Scott-Kemmis

2010). *Citizen Kane* by Orson Welles serves as a good example to understand the thin line separating success and failure in the movie industry. First released in 1941, *Citizen Kane* was lauded by critics but not the general audience, and it failed to recoup its costs. However, it attained classic status after getting favourable reviews in France and was re-released. Orson Welles, the producer and director, did not truly enjoy the success of this movie until later in life. However, Welles went on to create other movies despite being viewed as an outsider by the studio system. A similar example from the Indian movie industry is a classic movie titled *Mera Naam Joker* (*My Name Is Joker*) by one of the greatest showmen of Indian cinema, Raj Kapoor. First released in 1970, *Mera Naam Joker* was rejected by the audience and critics and it was condemned for both its content and its length. It caused severe financial strain on the producer/director Raj Kapoor and he was on the verge of bankruptcy. Though the movie is referred to as a cult classic today, with its music topping the all-time great lists and being feted extensively in the erstwhile Soviet Union, the bottom line was that it was a financial disaster. Kapoor did not lose heart and continued producing movies. His comeback was memorable when, in 1973, three years after the *Joker* debacle, he released *Bobby*, a teen romance which rewrote the rules of romance in Indian cinema and became a blockbuster. Though both Welles and Kapoor were affected by and paid the price for the box office's fickle-mindedness, they are perfect examples of resilience.

In the domains of management and psychology, researchers have shown a high degree of interest and curiosity in analysing how individuals come to terms with failure and stage comebacks from complicated and disappointing life situations (Bonanno, Rennicke and Dekel 2005). The broad spectrum of such studies comes under the umbrella of 'resilience' (Earvolino-Ramirez 2007). The English word resilience comes from the Latin word 'resilio', which, in a literal sense, means to jump back (Klein, Nicholls and Thomalla 2003). Tugade and Fredrickson (2004, p. 320) defined resilience as 'effective coping and adaptation, although faced with loss, hardship or adversity'. Without producers who exhibit a high degree of resilience, the movie industry would struggle to continue due to the high rate of failure. A producer who takes a blockbuster and a disaster in his or her stride can build an organisation and a body of work that stands the test of time, thereby creating an entrepreneurial legacy.

The next chapter presents the future of entrepreneurship in the Indian movie industry.

References

Bonanno, GA, Rennicke, C and Dekel, S 2005, 'Self-enhancement among high-exposure survivors of the September 11th terrorist attack: Resilience or social maladjustment?', *Journal of Personality and Social Psychology*, vol. 88, no. 6, pp. 984–998.

Earvolino-Ramirez, M 2007, 'Resilience: A concept analysis', *Nursing Forum*, vol. 42, no. 2, pp. 73–82.

Klein, RJT, Nicholls, RJ and Thomalla, F 2003, 'Resilience to natural hazards: How useful is this concept?', *Global Environmental Change Part B: Environmental Hazards*, vol. 5, no. 1, pp. 35–45.

Sardana, D and Scott-Kemmis, D 2010, 'Who learns what? A study based on entrepreneurs from biotechnology new ventures', *Journal of Small Business Management*, vol. 48, no. 3, pp. 441–468.

Shepherd, DA and Patzelt, H 2017, Researching entrepreneurships' role in sustainable development. in *Trailblazing in entrepreneurship*, pp. 149–179, Palgrave Macmillan, Cham.

Tugade, MM and Fredrickson, BL 2004, 'Resilient individuals use positive emotions to bounce back from negative emotional experiences', *Journal of Personality and Social Psychology*, vol. 86, no. 2, pp. 320–333.

7

THE FUTURE OF ENTREPRENEURSHIP IN INDIAN CINEMA

Closing credits

The movie business is a big gamble.

Jackie Chan, prolific action-movie star

I know there is one kind of cinema that exists in the world, that is good or bad cinema.

Raj Kapoor, the original Indian showman

Introduction

Jackie Chan, a cinema legend with roots in one of the most prolific movie industries in the world, speaks of the movie business a gamble because of its unpredictability: no one has deciphered exactly what works for the audience and for how long. Rather than blaming this unpredictability on the fickle-mindedness of the audience, it would be better to look inward and analyse the entreprenurial models of movie producers. The preceding chapters have presented Indian cinema through different lenses; however, the lens of the movie producer as entrepreneur is the most captivating. A creative, artistic medium such as cinema can only survive if there is a commercial element to it —and this is provided by the entrepreneurial producer. This chapter distils the insights of entrepreneurial Indian movie producers and their circle in order to examine the future challenges and opportunities which, if enacted, will see the industry thrive. Examining the movie producer as an entrepreneur who could achieve future success in and for the industry means assessing the contextual factors that may influence the future of Indian cinema. We also examine the key facets of an entrepreneurial Indian movie producer and consider the future of entrepreneurial Indian movie production.

Contextual factors and entrepreneurial Indian movie producers

Entrepreneurial Indian movie producers work under conditions of uncertainty (Hausmann 2010) since the nature of the market makes it extremely difficult to establish oneself as a movie producer. There are intrinsic contextual factors in play. A movie producer must have a wide range of skills and qualities, including the ability to innovate, a willingness to take risks and a pro-active attitude along with skills in business, law, negotiation, psychology and technology. But there is more to it. Risk-taking can turn into an obsession for control and a blind passion for product and process in moviemaking. When combined, these traits can facilitate or inhibit success, depending on how they are managed. Indian movie producers are prone to drive themselves to the point where passion sometimes boils over into obsession. Entrepreneurial Indian movie producers can be short-sighted, overly self-confident and independent but often need to self-improve by learning the business skills that will bring them the success they crave. Some have large egos. Others are mentors and coaches of the next generation of entrepreneurial Indian movie producers. But very few have formal training or education in the business of becoming an entrepreneurial Indian movie producer. As we have seen, the need for education about the business side of the industry has limited the reach and longevity of many enterprises. In the case of independent movie producers working in small businesses—often family-owned—these functions are undertaken by the founder. However, if a producer wants to produce a movie for mainly creative reasons, they may find they have limited business skills necessary to procure markets or manage the risks involved (Hausmann 2010). How many of them seek business advice when looking to produce a new movie? Of the 45 Indian movie producers and their circle interviewed for this book, only 10 per cent sought advice from traditional business experts like accountants, financial experts or consultants, putting themselves at greater risk of failure. These are internal contextual factors which are discussed below.

External contextual factors are also important. They include demand for the product, competitiveness of the environment, the possible oversupply of product in the movie industry and the turbulence and uncertainty of the wider world economy. In the volatile global market for Indian movies, the entertainment sector can be affected suddenly by a reluctance to spend if and when the economy plummets. Nonetheless, there is some good news. While the external environment is difficult at best, and there is no end in sight to the crises and financial troubles on the world stage that have a knock-on effect on the entertainment industries, entrepreneurial Indian movie producers are resilient, passionate and purposeful. They persist in the face of failure and remain dogged in the quest for success.

The future of entrepreneurship in Indian cinema

It is widely acknowledged that a nation's entrepreneurial activity is an indicator of the wealth and employment creation occurring in that nation. Indian cinema cannot rest on the accolades of being the largest market in terms of volume; it has to enhance the quality of products rather than churning out a large volume of inferior movies. In 1991, the Indian economy ushered in a set of reforms and opened up the insular economy in a popular move referred to as liberalisation. This spurred the economy on to a faster growth trajectory of almost 7 per cent per annum, regularly, over the past two decades. However, opening up the economy presented its own set of challenges, and one of the key realisations was that for India to be a globally integrated economy, entrepreneurship must be an important pathway towards this. The Indian movie industry has begun its journey but has still not developed the distinct core competencies it needs to set it apart from other movie industries, the volume of its output notwithstanding. This volume predominantly caters to the local market and the global diaspora. Catering to this market alone limits the potential of the Indian movie industry, meaning it will not be able to transcend its boundaries.

In order to become a significant player in the world market, like Hollywood, the Indian movie industry needs to develop content that attracts global viewership transcending geographic boundaries. The influence enjoyed by Hollywood has been criticised as cultural imperialism (Moody 2017) in some quarters but it has ensured the birth, growth and sustenance of several global organisations. The Indian movie industry's goal should be to emulate and better the Hollywood model in building global entertainment corporations that have a significant impact on world culture. The emphasis in the Indian movie industry is shifting towards the development of entrepreneurial skills so that a professional approach pervades the moviemaking business, making it more sustainable. Apart from creating substantial revenue growth and enhanced job opportunities for the Indian movie industry, it will also change the model of global aspiration for Indian movie producers. Entrepreneurial development programmes are supplementing existing mechanisms with the main objective of achieving these goals. Indian economic policy can be formulated in such a way, keeping in mind the funding required to support the development of entrepreneurship that could help with this global ambition. Once the policy template is fine-tuned, it can become a model for other movie industries aiming to encourage and develop movie producers' entrepreneurial activity.

An exciting pathway for Indian cinema in the future is the opening up of different avenues for showcasing content. Producers are pushing their entrepreneurial potential along with the advent of Amazon Prime, Netflix and other streaming platforms that offer an opportunity to showcase content without being constrained by the shackles of theatrical exhibition. The growing numbers of the Indian diaspora across the world ensure that there is demand for content on these globally mounted platforms. This could pave way for content that is refreshing and thought-provoking, thereby moving away from the song-and-dance formula. Additionally, star power might also diminish to some extent if movies are content-driven rather than seen as star vehicles. Though product placement and endorsements offer an opportunity for producers to explore additional revenue streams, they might be limited in scope.

Internationalisation in the true sense can be an exciting pathway for Indian producers, but ought not to mean simply releasing the same content in different markets, as discussed earlier, but should address the manner in which Indian producers might venture into producing foreign language movies by contributing their intellect as part of the culture of internationalisation (Geursen and Dana 2001). It might not be too long before Indian producers start producing movies in Spanish or French, for example.

Last year, Rajeev was at the premiere of a serious movie based on true events and noticed a couple walking out of the movie, commenting that it was too serious. They were expecting a light-hearted Bollywood movie with singing and dancing. Such a chance encounter makes you stop and think. How does the world perceive Indian cinema? For an industry that has celebrated a century of existence, it is surprising that the perception is narrow and only fits a single mould, thereby restricting its global reach. Another point worth mentioning is that during the 2019 Cannes Film Festival there was not a single movie from India. There were several leading ladies from the Indian movie industry walking the red carpet to enhance the fashion quotient, but not one movie. In the popular section, the retrospective portion, and in competition, there was not one solitary Indian movie. Surely an industry that churns out more than 2,000 movies per year can come up with one movie that is worthy of exhibition at Cannes? This is an unfortunate truth and reinforces the negative perception that Indian cinema is all about glitz and glamour but not serious content. But does it also say something about others' perceptions of movies that emerge from production centres beyond Hollywood? Despite the refreshing recent Oscar success of the South Korean Best Picture winner, *Parasite*, is there resistance in other parts of the world to recognising movies of a different genre?

Certainly, it takes time to build a profile as a serious content creator. Though there have been exceptions like Satyajit Ray and Adoor Gopalakrishnan, their movies were representing a very small niche of Indian cinema. To enhance credibility and gain global acceptance, Indian cinema needs to seamlessly integrate box office demands and creativity. Hollywood has proved it can be done. If the Italian and French movie industries, producing fewer than 50 movies per year, can win 20 Academy Awards (Radu 2019), then surely the Indian movie industry, with more than 2,000 movies per year (CBFC India 2017), can achieve commercial and critical respect across the world. Other countries like Australia have a small movie industry that contributes to the global cultural landscape. In fact, Australian cinema, despite existing for more than 100 years, had to suffer the indignity of being viewed as inferior to Hollywood for many years until ground-breaking scripts and projects altered that perception. Despite Indian moviemakers attending Cannes and other high-profile movie festivals every year, it is surprising they are not learning from the other successful business models present at Cannes and using that knowledge to better their industry. In the words of one producer, who treats Cannes as his annual learning expedition:

> I go to Cannes and other movie festivals because of my interest in the movie industry. I go there to meet people and to learn from them. The movie festival is a place where, that's why it is called a festival. Festival means, celebrating, meeting ten people connected with cinema. They bring in ideas. I listen to their perspective, their point of view. Every year the whole taste of cinema keeps changing. Evolving is a process; it keeps changing, even in Hollywood it keeps changing. I always try to learn and do something different from others. Only then do you get noticed.

'Being noticed' has to be the mantra for the Indian movie industry. It has to be the rallying call for all the creators so that they can focus on content that will get noticed. It might be difficult to make every movie very high quality, and difficult for the hundreds of movies that are released every year in India to be noticed, but there should be a groundswell where producers realise the importance of quality and join the movement to be noticed. Today, any movie produced by George Lucas or Steven Spielberg is noticed because the audience, distributors, exhibitors and critics expect it to be of a certain quality and they believe in the capabilities of these creators.

There needs to be a talent pool that is adept at creating such high quality work. Movie producers are the entrepreneurs who can fulfil the role of catalyst for this transformation process. Such transformation can fuel growth in the industry and thereby contribute to economic development. But to achieve the transformation of Indian cinema, Indian movie producers need to be trained, developed and educated in the skills required for movie production success. Unfortunately, there is a surprisingly high degree of resistance to this notion amongst movie producers. As one experienced producer, eager to mentor new producers, lamented, the lack of initiative and interest from new producers to learn was of great concern to him:

> My biggest concern today is that producers do not want to learn from other failures; they want to learn from their own failures. Their ego is so big that they think they know everything. They don't want to approach you. They don't want to ask you if it is right or wrong or if they can do anything different.

Personal traits such as size of ego are seen to be barriers to learning, according to this producer. There is also resistance to understanding the financial aspects and efficient use of resources for movie production.

Financial mismanagement: they don't understand. Every individual project has to make money or lose money. They are prepared to increase their risk exposure by running multiple projects. That does not work well in cinema. At the end of the day one loss will pull you down and cause the business to collapse. A lot of production houses collapse because they are not prepared for the future; they only think of today.

Furthermore, new young producers want to come into the business and start without training and development, or indeed experience. This has created a sense of apathy, disappointing experienced producers. One of these experienced producers commented:

The younger generation has spoilt the industry because of their lack of knowledge. They take decisions that are not well thought out. This has been detrimental to the industry. They have poor planning, poor execution and obviously end up with poor results. You need to have experienced and passionate people coming in so that there is a profit for everyone. It is a good business. If you are able to work well within the parameters, then it will work out well. Since I have faced so many knocks and setbacks, I am able to withstand them, and think of the future. This is because of my experience. There are many newcomers who come in unprepared and exit after just one setback.

Unfortunately, breakdown and loss of money is the ultimate price paid by an untrained and unprepared movie producer, and they leave the industry after just one movie. Exiting after just one production means that the financial losses and the emotional strain are high and the producer may be unable to withstand it. The producer cannot contemplate learning and improving because the experience has been so bad that only withdrawal seems possible. As one leading actor who branched out into movie production through his production house commented:

Is it correct to become a producer without any experience or training? Here a producer is considered a financier. Actually, a producer is the one who designs the project, designs the script, and who assembles the cast and crew. Unfortunately, here it has changed, always the producer is on the backstage where they only give money and pay for the daily expenses.

As seen in comments above, there is also concern that new entrants are not adept at financial management, which has a negative impact on the production, on the set and in terms of team spirit. This is seen to be a 'bad model' that affects entrepreneurial success:

Producing a movie here, the knowledge is zero, you don't have to acquire knowledge to produce a movie. This is a bad model. Many producers don't want to acquire and share knowledge and responsibility with anybody. When this is the case, the producer becomes a financier. They borrow money from a financier, and they invest in the movie. Technically speaking, there is no right model of how to train a producer in India. How well you can manage your funds to shoot that day is purely up to the producer.

Despite clearly identifying the problem of producers losing control, new entrants in the industry do not tap into the expertise available to avoid mistakes. In short, entrepreneurs in the movie business in India fly by the seat of their pants more often than not.

Avoiding mistakes is an entrepreneurial learning process that will aid in the development of a new type of entrepreneur. One producer, who was offering advice to many leading actors and who then moved into movie production, suggested that new entrants in the movie business:

> ... would be taken for a ride. Any new movie producer, whether he is big or small, I am sure the industry will take him for a ride. It is the same now as it was 16 years ago, if you have no knowledge of movie production.

So, if a newcomer refuses to undertake formal training, how will they learn the nitty-gritty? One way is by joining up with another production house, learning by observing and working at every possible role on the set.

A young producer who has just started dipping his toes into production after working under a very senior producer for many years, has this to say about how he was mentored and coached by a senior producer:

> Every day is an experience where I learn from mistakes, but learning means learning correctly from the senior producer. When I was with him, it was real learning for me; it might sound like a very old formula, but that was real learning, it was the golden formula for success. Many old production houses are not making movies today because of not adhering to the golden formula. I commenced my career as a producer with the clear intention of bringing in financial discipline of my mentor the senior producer.

Intuitively, it makes sense to either get formal or informal training before embarking on the production journey, because of the financial risks involved. But it is surprising that many new and aspiring producers ignore this, ending up making costly mistakes. If not academic or formal training, there needs to be a period of coaching and mentoring to help a new aspirant understand the production process and even help them make a decision as to whether this is the right field and choice for them. This will help them make an educated decision rather than going in blind without an inkling of what the entire process entails.

Certainly, the process can be taught in a media or movie school. But a large number of producers take the view that the ability to come up with solutions in tricky situations has to be developed by the individual and fine-tuned with experience. This belief is what is holding the industry back from young producers undertaking training, development or education. This point of view is emphatically pointed out by one producer:

> Training and education of a producer cannot be done academically, a movie school cannot teach you to be a producer; the producer's role is like managing human emotions. New producers come in with cash bags and they learn from their own mistakes. They can talk to me and learn from my experience, but they prefer to do it on their own. When you tell somebody that movie has to be done in this style and shape it will not make any sense to them, and they will not take it in the right way.

If producers cannot take responsibility for their shortcomings, who can? Blaming the ecosystem does not work because it is made up of producers and other stakeholders. Therefore, the shortcomings of the producers enter into the ecosystem in which they operate and dent its credibility, dampening the enthusiasm of professionals who want to establish a career path in the movie industry.

One of the main objectives of a producer who is also a senior office-bearer in the producers' council—the highest body that oversees industry development—is to make the field attractive for newcomers and professionals to opt for it as a career option. Accordingly, he is introducing a form of training to the council:

> For newcomers, I am trying to bring in a basic model through the council, so that people will come and learn. Now I am lending my experience to the producers who are willing to take it. My advice is anybody who comes into this business has to stick to the content; they have to learn first before getting into production. Because our product is not something which is like a tangible product, it is an intangible product. We sell ideas, in the form of stories and concepts and we have to make sure that we sell unique ideas; if we invest less on those ideas, we are not successful. When we fail, we have to fail small and when we succeed, we have to succeed big time.

The need for training and development is a sentiment echoed by a second-generation producer who is ready to pass the baton to the next generation:

How can my experience benefit youngsters who come into the industry? Success is ok, but how to handle failure? They have to, one thing I strongly feel is that I am not discouraging new people from coming into the industry. I am sure new people with new ideas can come, this is very important for the future of the industry. My sons are learning from me; they are on the sets throughout. They are there for every shot. I make it a point and till the end of my life as long as I am in the industry, I will definitely be there on the shooting spot. I don't get involved creatively but you know to plan for the next day, planning for the schedule, in support for the director, I am there.

There is some recognition of the need to change and that is about providing learning opportunities for the next generation of movie producers. Support is a crucial word in the entrepreneurial lexicon, and it can come from the government offering training programmes, incentives and grants for new entrepreneurs; from independent organisations like movie corporations, incubators and accelerators that bring investors, entrepreneurs and mentors together; or from industry bodies like the movie chamber, producers' guild or producers' associations. A senior producer who was heading one of the oldest industry chambers lamented that it was well-nigh impossible to change things in relation to training and development:

Nobody listens to what we say, they don't want to listen but one thing is true, in this industry the guy who starts from the bottom and slowly climbs up the steps of success stays longest in the industry and the guys who come in intermittently with money bags will exit in the middle; they will not stay for long. I have tried to reason with many newcomers and bring them into realisation about the nature of this industry and the resilience they need to have. Even when I was the president of the chamber, I used to advise them saying that if they do not understand the nitty-gritty of production, then they will not be able to withstand the rigours of this industry. Behaviour, discipline and credibility are extremely important.

This producer adds that the glamour trap that can entice young players into the industry gets in the way of the need for training and development:

Which business gives them the chance to be on TV for 30 minutes? Which business gives them the opportunity to be in all the newspapers? Only in the cinema industry, even without education and formal qualifications, this industry allows you to come in and go much ahead than many people who are well qualified, that is the glamour of the cinema industry.

The glamour of the cinema industry is the elephant in the room, and though no producer has directly acknowledged or accepted this fact, it is worth discussing. Is glamour one of the motivating factors for new entrants into movie production? This young producer sums it up succinctly:

> I know that it is not possible to have success throughout a lifetime. That is a rare percentage for one in a million people. It is God's gift to taste that success. For everyone else, it is a journey of ups and downs. The problem here is what their understanding of cinema is—that is a very big question. Why they are coming to cinema is a very big question. Some people come into cinema to earn money, some people come into cinema to earn fame, and some people come into cinema to act.

This producer continues to explain how the entrepreneurial background of a movie producer is relevant and might even be the reason for their resistance to training:

> When I came to cinema, I had succeeded in my business and applied the same principles in this business; everyone should do that. There are many producers with a successful entrepreneurial background entering movie production, but when they are entering the industry; they are successful business guys so they will not listen to advice because they are coming from a successful background and psychologically, they are not prepared to listen. They see you as a competitor, only they think: why should only you make a movie they can also make? In cinema you need to know the logistics after the release, how to get back your money and recover your investment. That is a valuable lesson in this business.

Underlying these conversations about the need for training and development is competition rather than collaboration. The producers and their circle are still in the competition phase, not recognising the benefits of collaboration that may take the industry forward. Valuable lessons shape the entrepreneurial journey of movie producers. If they learn from those lessons and do necessary course correction in a time-bound manner, their chances of survival and success rise. If they fail to learn and continue chasing dreams with unrealistic expectations, they will be forced to exit the industry. Such forced exits will dent the reputation of the Indian movie industry more than shattered dreams and financial losses. Quality becomes the first casualty. Every producer wants to stick to a formula that will increase the chance of success. For the Indian movie industry to succeed and become a robust hub of entrepreneurial activity, basic principles need to be laid out and adhered to.

Entrepreneurial Indian movie producers

Entrepreneurial movie producers can be divided into different categories depending on the purpose of the enterprise they lead, the movie producers participating in it, and the entrepreneurial functions undertaken. They are motivated by the drive to realise a creative concept, the need for independence in employment, the will to pursue a specific assignment and frustration with others not being prepared to pursue their vision.

According to the Global Entrepreneurship Monitor, entrepreneurs' motivations can be divided into two categories: opportunity and necessity (Mota, Braga and Ratten 2019). The pull of opportunity and the push of necessity (Van der Zwan et al. 2016) can be reasons for entrepreneurs to enter into movie production. It is essential to understand the role played by motivation in creating new production houses or organisations in the movie industry. All the second-generation producers had the necessity of running an existing business and turning it around from the verge of bankruptcy or using the platform as an opportunity to expand and grow the business. In other words, they were either pushed into the industry to safeguard family interests or the industry pulled them in as an attractive career choice. There are movie producers who get into the business as a choice, i.e., an opportunity—they choose to enter it due to necessity or an interest that encourages them to shift from a different industry to the movie industry. A producer who was an architect and operated a successful architecture firm describes his transition to movie producer:

> I became an architect. Then I wanted to own a firm. I started one. I was 24 when I started my own architectural practice. Our practice flourished. We won numerous awards in architecture. Thrice we won the best architect of the year award in the entire country. I was getting claustrophobic. Since I decided to practice in a certain city, the city gave me opportunities. Strangely, I was doing a movie; I was doing a design for a leading actor's house. I was being extremely experimental. I thought it was a great opportunity for me to do something big. Sadly, those designs were not taken up. That gave me the calling, it hit me, and I had to move on. I wanted to be a movie maker. I was creatively inclined and commenced work as a producer.

A similar experience is shared by another producer, who was a successful travel businessman:

> I was in the travel business. I was a package tour operator before I came into this industry. It was a family business. I expanded it to the international level. At that time, I was contemplating starting another business so that I could grow as an individual as well as in my career. The main reason I entered the cinema is that there is an abundant labour supply and for the correct price. If I choose the correct set of people, they are working for me as well as for themselves.

Does the fear of failure haunt Indian movie producers, or do they exude confidence in their ability to produce successful movies? The interviews undertaken provide some conclusions. Most of the Indian movie producers wished to remain independent movie producers. They continue to have the courage to navigate the challenges of the Indian movie market. They remain optimistic about future prospects despite the volatility of the global marketplace and the uncertainty of tapping into the needs of movie audiences. What then are the main determinants of success for the Indian movie producer? They seem to be the following matters: personal contacts in a South Asian nation where connections are paramount to success, at least in terms of having the movie concept taken to the implementation stage; the ability to mix creative vision with business expertise in the moviemaking process; and sound planning and organisation. Of course, these factors take for granted that the core creative idea is sound and that the finances are in place. Interestingly, other studies of cultural entrepreneurs have confirmed these tentative results (e.g., Hausmann 2010). Thus, we conclude that the personal qualities of the Indian movie entrepreneur play a decisive role in their success or failure. That said, contextual factors affect the success or failure of Indian movie entrepreneurs. Clearly, when conditions in the environment are challenging, additional hurdles for the entrepreneur are created, and such obstacles could well lead to failure. The need for training and development is one such factor that spans the personal and the contextual.

Reading these examples of Indian producers' craving for independence presents an interesting exploration into why they chose the path of entrepreneurship, especially in the creative field of moviemaking. The two examples quoted above are of producers who ran businesses successfully before entering the movie business. They had developed entrepreneurial businesses that honed their skills in calculated entrepreneurial venturing, risk-taking and innovativeness. Furthermore, they were creative individuals, had developed business skills in another domain (which was essentially a training ground for their future endeavours) and became successful movie producers. In short, they combined creative vision with business acumen in running a small to medium-sized enterprise, managing finances and managing teams of people. Analysing the career trajectories of legendary movie entrepreneurs like Darryl F. Zanuck, Sam Goldwyn and Walt Disney reveals that they chose movies as their medium for entrepreneurship after working in other domains like hospitality (Zanuck), apparel (Goldwyn) and illustrations (Disney). In their earlier non-entrepreneurial days, the above-mentioned entrepreneurs assessed their lives (Obodaru 2012) and were not satisfied with the outcome, prompting them to change their life paths and become entrepreneurs. Had they been satisfied, the movie world in particular, and the cultural landscape in general, would have missed out on their contributions. Therefore, whether movie producers chose the entrepreneurial pathway of movie production due to necessity, or due to family responsibility, or due to a career choice, or due to passion, it is evident that the challenges they face are similar and there is no magic formula for success. It is a combination of careful script selection, prudent budgeting, effective project management and innovative marketing that increases their chances of success. At the end of the day, success determines the survival of a movie producer and having a *Ben Hur* or a *Baahubali* on their résumé will go a long way in ensuring their survival.

Independence is one of the most cherished facets or ideals of an entrepreneur (Van der Zwan et al. 2016). A movie producer tends to have the heaviest workload of all the technicians, cast and crew involved in movie production. As evident from the remarks of a senior producer: 'The 7 a.m. call sheet means, I used to be at the location at 6.30am. I am there throughout shoot time; I used to push the trolley, hold the crane, work in the shooting spot.'

A dedicated producer has limited time for rest and relaxation because every department is under their control. This yearning for independence is very high in a movie producer and can at some point act as abarrier to seeking necessary professional help. Nonetheless, this independence has been crucial for producers, right from Samuel Goldwyn to Aditya Chopra: they will not compromise on their autonomy. An entrepreneur takes pride in the sense of achievement—it is very evident in a movie producer who desires both awards (artistic excellence) as well as rewards (financial returns). There are several examples to highlight the entrepreneur's obsession with control and movie producers are no exception to this trait. Whether it is Zanuck or Lucas, stories abound about their tendency to micromanage and this was also very evident in Indian movie producers like Raj Kapoor and AVM who controlled every moving part and also took the key risks.

Where next for Indian movie producers?

Is there good cinema or bad cinema? Or do we agree with the popular belief that there is no good cinema or bad cinema but just hits or flops? Ultimately, movies need to be commercially viable so that the livelihoods of cast, crew and the supporting structures of the establishment can sustain themselves. Indian cinema has often been derided for not being intellectual enough and for pandering to the lowest possible denominator of taste. This criticism stems from the fact that there is not a single winner from India in the Best Foreign Language movie category of the Academy Awards. But is this is the correct gauge for measuring success? According to the Academy of Motion Picture Arts and Sciences database, Italy and France have won 20 awards between them (awardsdatabase.org), whereas China, Hong Kong and India have won none. Employing this measure to denigrate two of the largest movie industries in the world would be very unfair. Cinema can be analysed from an intellectual standpoint so that it holds up against other creative arts, but what about entertainment? Cinema from Hong Kong, China and India tends to be hugely popular and entertaining; does that mean entertainment is a lower virtue as compared to intellectual stimulation? If so, so be it. Viewed against the backdrop of the two most populous nations in the world, cinema is the cheapest form of entertainment and a form of escape from the drudgery, chaos and daily grind that surrounds the citizens of these nations. If Yash Chopra drapes his leading ladies in white and makes them sing and dance in the rather alluring locations of Switzerland, it is to entertain and to provide an escape from drudgery for many an Indian viewer. If Ang Lee makes his leading lady fly through the air and vanquish evil forces, it is to entertain and to provide a flight of fancy from a tough life for many a Chinese viewer. Therefore, applying the same yardstick of quality to European, Chinese and Indian cinema cannot be justified.

If box office success is a yardstick for measuring the quality of cinema, then the percentage of success in Hollywood is almost on a par with the percentage of success in Indian or, indeed, Chinese cinema. The failure rate in Indian moviemaking is high, and some producers say it is as high as 90 per cent. In the words of the former president of a leading trade body:

> Nowadays the success rate of Indian movies is hardly 10 per cent, and the regional Indian movies is hardly 5 per cent. That is too much of a burden. If it was a failure in the olden days, we recovered 50 per cent of the cost at least but nowadays we lose 100 to 125 per cent of our investment.

There is a dearth of research on movie entrepreneurs, despite the significant cultural and economic impact of the movie industry. Annual turnover in the movie industry is $38.6 billion globally, projected to reach $50 billion by 2020, and it employs more than two million people in the US alone (MPAA, 2017). Yet fewer than 20 per cent of movies are successful (Sparviero 2015), so entrepreneurial failure is pervasive in this industry.

Failure is pervasive and very frequent, but why do movie producers continue to make movies rather than exit the industry? Passion is a common theme that keeps recurring in all our conversations with movie producers. A majority of movie producers cited passion as the main factor that pushed them to battle the odds and keep going despite failures. Though on the surface a movie producer might seem to be at peace with the process of movie production or, in other words, exhibit harmonious passion (Vallerand 2015), underneath the surface there is a strong hint of obsessiveness (Fisher, Merlot and Johnson 2018). As noted in the earlier chapters, there are producers at both ends of the spectrum, from harmonious to obsessive. Passion drives the producers to be critical of themselves and their work and, interestingly, many producers gave themselves a low score in terms of their lifetime achievement, despite being in the industry for a long period. One producer even compared himself with a 'kindergarten kid' because he feels learning is continuous in the industry. Interestingly, he uses a cricketing analogy (another Indian obsession!) to describe how he sees himself:

> In this long innings, I don't see myself as a success or failure, but I am still in kindergarten. I am learning because we make a movie and we don't know whether it will run or be sold out. The day we know that the first show will be sold out, is when we enter the first grade. We are making movies with the understanding that people might come and watch them. We cannot predict people's taste; we cannot predict the future of the movie.

Predicting the success of a movie has not been perfected by anyone in the world; the biggest names in the movie industry have had their share of disasters, but they moved onto bigger projects and ensured that the same mistakes were not repeated. As one producer points out, surviving itself is success in the movie industry:

> At least if you are better in every movie, somewhere your journey will be better, somewhere your journey will be more profitable and at the end, it will be more memorable. I put it this way, in the cinema industry, survival itself is a success, a lot of people have come before me, a lot of people came when I was there, a lot of people came after me, and they all left. They all left. I am still there.

Another producer called himself a 'zero' because of not achieving anything significant, suggesting that producers tend to measure themselves against tough yardsticks:

> I have been in the industry for close to 24 years. Till now, I have not achieved anything; independently I have not achieved much. I started my own banner and even though I have set up my own company and produced movies, I have not released a movie on my own. I have to release on my own and establish a name in the market and then I can measure my success. Till then I am a zero.

Yet another established producer who has produced more than 30 movies, refused to even award a score for his achievement: 'As a report card, I have just started to not even pass because just the schooling is over; it is a learning process. So, I cannot give myself a score.'

After 30 movies, if this producer feels he has just commenced his journey, then it indicates a steep learning curve or a deep passion for the industry that prompts such humility. The learning curve occurs from self-teaching and the passion works best if harnessed by business knowledge.

Apart from passion, movie producers attribute their lineage or parental influence as a factor that prompted them to take up production as an entrepreneurial pathway. Family connections or parents operating a successful production house offer an opportunity for the second or third generation to continue the business without going through the rigours of a start-up—though they may face other challenges. The experience of a second-generation producer who is now handing over the reins to the third generation is interesting:

> My father and his partners were pioneers in movie production. They started their careers in the late 1950s and early 1960s until the 1970s. They made several movies under their production banner. They produced several blockbusters and worked with superstars of that generation. I didn't have much of an interest in moviemaking. My mother insisted that I should get back to my hometown and sort out our family business affairs, because in the three years I was away, my father and father's partner's company was on the verge of bankruptcy. Their organisation expanded but subsequently they had a few failures; big failures. Unfortunately, they got into the wrong projects and lost a lot of money. My mother said that I had to get back and sort out the financial mess. That is how I ended up a movie producer.

This is an interesting example because this producer was not initially keen to get into the family business and was pursuing a professional career. However, circumstances forced him to take up the mantle of producer. Another producer recounts his early initiation into the world of movie production:

> I was introduced: I started looking after [things], right from the age of 12, I used to go with my father, and I used to go to the editing suite. I'd take the splicer, cut, stick, and sync the sound, it was something nice and creative, I used to pass it and run through the edit. I was doing that when I was 12 years old and 13 years old. Then slowly I started going into the production process and this made me learn the intricacies of movie production very early in life.

This producer was a willing participant whereas the previous producer was forced to get into the business due to family circumstances, and there is another type of producer who is like a reluctant debutante. Such reluctance could be due to resistance from the first-generation producer themself or from the second generation. There are even instances of the first generation refusing to let their children enter into the business but the second generation fighting to enter, as is evident from the words of this second-generation producer:

My father did not want me to come into this industry and he thought that I would change my mind and go to the US and do a Master's in Science degree—all such regular things. But for me, it was not the right thing, it took two years for me to convince my dad that I had to be in this industry, so finally he started the recording studio for me.

Risk-taking is an inherent quality in many producers. In fact, if there were no penchant for risk-taking, movies would not have evolved from silents to talkies, to colour pictures, to 70 mm, to 3D. However, it has to be noted that entrepreneurs don't just exhibit a willingness to take risks; they actively go looking for them. Several examples of turnaround specialists highlight this fact. Such entrepreneurs actively seek risk by picking up organisations that are bankrupt and turn them around into successful operations. Rajeev has personally interacted with several producers who literally placed their house on the line by borrowing significant sums of money with the hope that their next production would be a blockbuster. Such producers tend to lose sight of the long-term objective and focus on the short-term, production-to-production cycle. This might be one of the reasons that explains the absence of any production house in India that has lasted more than 100 years.

Many producers tend to avoid seeking new opportunities because of this short-sightedness, and they would prefer to operate within the comfortable confines of a formula, and stick to it rather than change it, so that they can continue enjoying success. However, by the time the formula is rejected by the audience, the producer has lost touch with the audience and will struggle to succeed. Some producers manage to strike a balance between sticking to the formula and creating a new formula; such producers enjoy longer periods of success and higher chances of surviving over generations. Similarly, producers in the movie industry tend to be laggards when it comes to innovation, and this is more pronounced in the Indian movie industry, which is still stuck in the formulaic-content zone with a certain number of songs and fights that get in the way of the narrative. Although this trend is changing, there is still a long way to go. A true entrepreneur is innovative by nature, spotting a chance for success and focusing on it. There are a few innovative movie producers with mixed bags of success and failure—some were labelled as being too far ahead of their time, which dents the self-confidence of such innovative producers.

Self-confidence is an essential trait for every entrepreneur—confidence that leads them to believe in their abilities and confidence that leads them to commit to projects and execute them successfully. However, this self-confidence can quickly become a negative trait when they refuse to acknowledge reality and become delusional in their beliefs about their ability to execute a new venture well. The high number of movies stuck in cans, awaiting release, highlights this delusional trait in many movie producers who get into the business without a proper understanding of the reality and then get stuck midway. Apart from the motivation for success, financial rewards and intellectual glory, a movie producer who enjoys the work of production rather than viewing it as a chore tends to last longer, and is motivated to launch new productions and build a strong production house. As detailed earlier in this chapter, most producers tend to resist conventional training in movie production; this might sound counter-intuitive, especially when high stakes and large amounts of money are involved, so a typical movie producer prefers learning on the job or some might learn vital skills by assisting other producers. While learning on the job they develop a vision for their own production style—it might not be visionary but simply a compilation of the best practices that worked well on the job. A majority of movie producers, in Indian cinema especially, lack long-term vision; their vision is restricted to launching the next project or scoring with that elusive blockbuster combination. They tend to be fanatical about blockbuster success, thereby sacrificing long-term vision. This fanatical approach is reflected in one producer's comment:

> The writer and I moved to the movie production hub, leaving our families behind, the children studying. We thought first let us settle down; production is not an ordinary thing, it is very risky. Let us try one or two ventures and then we will see.

This senior producer rose through the ranks from a production office manager to a distribution company partner and then a producer. This attitude is typical of a movie producer—they tend to get fanatical about launching new ventures and gladly or grudgingly sacrifice family life for achieving that goal. Our principal author Rajeev can vouch for the fact that, to make one movie, as a rule of thumb ten ideas are discussed, then four or five first drafts are looked into and, finally, three or four will make it to the full-bound script stage and of those one will be selected to commence the process of casting and principal photography. Despite this rigorous scrutiny, the high degree of failure (Sparviero 2015) in the movie business prevails. Hence, it is not surprising to observe fanatical traits in movie producers. One could argue that formal training in movie production and educating aspiring movie producers about the different motives for choosing movie production as an entrepreneurial pathway could help increase the chances of success; but it is surprising to see the degree of resistance to this idea.

Finally, there is a crying need for more female movie entrepreneurs. Although the global percentage is low, it is much lower in Indian cinema and, as indicated in Chapter 4, a significant majority of female Indian movie producers tend to be the wives and daughters of leading stars or producers. While further research is essential to understand this trend from a cultural and social perspective, it is evident that movie production should be presented as a viable career option for female entrepreneurs. As pointed out by the only female producer in this book:

Like they have seen me in production every day and observers used to comment that I managed very well and took care of everyone. You feel proud, though it might be momentary, I feel that it is the credibility I have built. That is the reason that my husband has won as the president of the actors' association. That is one of the credibility factors.

This female producer rates credibility as a very important trait and, with a sense of pride, states that she has built hers on her own. Such producers can be role models for other female producers to consider movie production as a viable career option. Though the number of female students enrolling in film and media courses in India is on the rise, the cascading effect of the increase in the number of females taking up roles behind the camera is not yet visible. With a population of close to half a billion women, only 14 per cent of entrepreneurs in India are women and this disparity is even starker in the Indian movie industry. With training and the opening up of entrepreneurial pathways for women in Indian movies, this figure is bound to change for better in the near future.

Conclusion

Despite more than 100 years of movie production, it is disappointing for Indian movie producers to still be searching for the status they desire. Many producers attempt to change, trying to create Indian movies that are on a par with global standards in terms of content and execution. But the world has not caught up with them either. Hollywood resists acknowledging foreign films, or indeed a foreign movie industry, despite its size and reach. Making movies might be a time-consuming process, but taking a helicopter view of where the future lies for entrepreneurial Indian movie producers depends on them stepping up to a higher level, as much as the world needs to come to them. The future of the industry depends on quality that matches world standards and not just quantity of output. The future of the industry depends on ensuring that the world changes its perception of the Indian movie industry so that it is seen as not just song and dance but a true entrepreneurial journey …

References

Academy of Motion Picture Arts and Sciences awards database, accessed 24/05/19, http://awardsdatabase.oscars.org.
Central Board of Movie Certification 2017, Ministry of Information and Broadcasting, Government of India. *Annual Report April 2016 to March 2017*, accessed 24/05/19, www.cbfcindia.gov.in/main/CBFC_English/Attachments/AR_2016-17_English.pdf.
Fisher, R, Merlot, E and Johnson, LW 2018, 'The obsessive and harmonious nature of entrepreneurial passion', *International Journal of Entrepreneurial Behaviour and Research*, vol. 24, no. 1, pp. 22–40.

Geursen, GM and Dana, LP 2001, 'International entrepreneurship: The concept of intellectual internationalisation', *Journal of Enterprising Culture*, vol. 9, no. 3, pp. 331–352.

Hausmann, A 2010, 'German artists between bohemian idealism and entrepreneurial dynamics', *International Journal of Arts Management*, vol. 12, no. 2, pp. 17–29.

Moody, P, 2017, 'US embassy support for Hollywood's global dominance: Cultural imperialism redux', *International Journal of Communication*, vol. 11, pp. 2912–2925.

Mota, A, Braga, V and Ratten, V 2019, 'Entrepreneurship motivation: Opportunity and necessity', in V Ratten, P Jones, V Braga and C Marques (eds), *Sustainable Entrepreneurship: Contributions to Management Science*, pp. 139–165, Springer, Switzerland AG.

Motion Picture Association of America 2017, *Theme (A Comprehensive Analysis and Survey of the Theatrical and Home Entertainment Market Environment) Report*, MPAA, Washington, DC.

Obodaru, O 2012, 'The self not taken: How alternative selves develop and how they influence our professional lives', *Academy of Management Review*, vol. vol. 37, no. 1, pp. pp. 34–57.

Radu, S 2019, 'Countries that have won the most Oscars', *USNews*, 21 February, accessed 24/05/19, https://www.usnews.com/news/best-countries/slideshows/countries-that-have-won-the-most-oscars.

Sparviero, S 2015, 'Hollywood creative accounting: The success rate of major motion pictures', *Media Industries Journal*, vol. 2, pp. 19–36.

Vallerand, RJ 2015, *The Psychology of Passion: A Dualistic Model*, Oxford University Press, New York.

Van der Zwan, P, Thurik, R, Verheul, I and Hessels, J 2016, 'Factors influencing the entrepreneurial engagement of opportunity and necessity entrepreneurs', *Eurasian Business Review*, vol. 6, no. 3, pp. 273–295.